THE NEW BOOK
OF THE DEAD

THE NEW BOOK
OF THE DEAD

The Initiate's Path into the Light

Dolores Ashcroft-Nowicki

Aquarian/Thorsons
An Imprint of HarperCollins*Publishers*

The Aquarian Press
An Imprint of HarperCollins*Publishers*
77–85 Fulham Palace Road,
Hammersmith, London W6 8JB

Published by The Aquarian Press 1992
1 3 5 7 9 10 8 6 4 2

A catalogue record for this book
is available from the British Library

ISBN 0 85030 951 4

Typeset by Harper Phototypesetters Limited,
Northampton, England
Printed in Great Britain by
Billings Bookplan Limited, Worcester

Contents

Dedication

To you, the one who has been with me constantly in this life and down through the centuries, guiding me and training for each life's work. I know you best as Anu, but you have had other names in your aeons long dealing with Humanity. This is your book for it deals with what has always been your particular work. One day I know that the Henu Boat will spread its wings for me, and that you will be at the helm.

Acknowledgements

This has not been an easy book to write and the research has been difficult, for death is not something people like to speak about freely. However I would like to thank the following:

Thames and Hudson for permission to quote from Alan Watts' book, *Myth and Ritual in Christianity*.

Michael as always for his encouragement and support, and his cooking!

Ann-Elisabeth Evason for her invaluable help in keeping things going while I slogged it out at the computer. Billie John for permission to use her drawings of Osiris, Thoth, Anubis, the procession of the Gods and the Ur-Hekau and Adze sceptres. David Goddard for his advice on matters pertaining to the viewpoint of the church and for seeking out odd bits of information I would otherwise have missed. J.H. 'Herbie' Brennan for always being there when I ring him up asking weird questions, and for listening to my screwball ideas for new books. Luke Dalton for invaluable help with research. I have learned and seen more than perhaps I wanted to know about the work of morticians and modern embalming methods during the writing of this book due to the kindness of many unnamed people. I realize that you would rather your names did not appear on this page, but I do thank you for you help and advice.

Introduction

Since I first thought about writing this book, many others on the same subject have been written about the process of death. Most of them have been looking at the phenomenon of passing from the layman's point of view. This book has been written from the perspective of the Western Mysteries.

Over the last thirty odd years the ancient mysteries have started to come into their own. Many schools and courses are now open to those seeking the old wisdom and offer good sound training in the occult sciences, in the Art of High Magic and Ritual, and in many of the disciplines encompassed by the word Mysteries. Dying, however, is not regarded as an Art, although it requires as much preparation and thought and, indeed, intention as does a ritual. I hope that in this book I have been able to point those who wish to prepare for this, the greatest of adventures, in the right direction.

We tend, in the West, to ignore death until it is right there in front of us; this does not allow long enough for things to be done in the right and suitable way for one who is a student of the Old Wisdom. Once you have made your arrangements there is a sense of having set things in motion for the moment that will come to us all. You also have the knowledge that you have left little for your family to cope with at a time when they will need support, rather than seeing to the innumerable details that crop up when someone dies.

If you do belong to a school, Order or Lodge, get your brethren together and discuss the points raised in this book. It is in such a context that any Lodge worth its Name and Symbol will find the depths of its fellowship. If a brother asks for help and assurance in these matters, it is a part of what you share together in Lodge that you offer as much help as you feel able to give. These are not discussions of gloom, but plans for entering into a new phase of Life.

No one wants to die, we all hope for long and happy lives with those we love, but we live in a world of uncertainty and danger, and must be prepared to go when we are called. Otherwise it will be too late to think of what you would have liked to have had arranged.

One of the gifts that Initiation into the Mysteries of Old gave to those entering its doors was the gift of the Knowledge of Immortality – not, you will notice, Immortality itself. That knowledge took away the fear, the dread, of death. I would be foolish indeed to say that this book will give you the same assurance, but I hope that what it will do is give you an idea of how it can be, and how you can combat the fear of death.

PART 1

THE BEARER
OF THE SCYTHE

1

The Ancient Enemy

All are but parts of one stupendous whole.
Whose body Nature is, and God the soul.
Alexander Pope, 1688–1744

Coming to Terms with Death

The one consistent element for all life on this planet, regardless of species, sex, status or environment, is the inevitability of death. Some fear it, some fear only the manner of its coming, all of us are fascinated by its secrets and what lies beyond its sunset barriers. Throughout history, attempts have been made to catch even the merest glimpse behind those barriers, to find some shred of hard evidence, some comforting assurance, however small, that death is not the end but some kind of new beginning. Some claim to have found it; others opt for blind faith or patent disbelief; most simply hope.

The great orthodox religions of the world have claimed the key to the understanding of death. They offer comfort and assurance to those who follow them, but for the most part, especially certain Christian sects, they take pains to point out that unless one follows their particular version of 'The One Truth', salvation and a new life will not be forthcoming. The message of Love and the doctrine of The Many Mansions preached by the gentle Nazarene Master is all too often lost amid evangelical promises of agonizing hellfire and eternal damnation for those living and believing outside the Christian faith. The Muslim faith also tends to be violent if you do not believe in its particular Prophet, so one faces coercion by fear on the one hand, and conversion by the sword on the other, with the Buddha's Middle Way neatly bisecting them. But what of those other paths, the minorities, the despised ones, those dispossessed of their right to believe as they wish by political and emotional pressure from the so-called orthodox religions. They take their faith from ancient ways and beliefs that trace back their beginnings beyond the memory of humanity. They too have their ways of death, their beliefs in a future life and manner of preparation for the last journey. Such beliefs and methods are just as valid, just as holy, and as full of promise for those who follow them. The Egyptians wrote a book of the Death Journey for their Initiates and those who believed in the Gods of their time, which they called *The Book of the Coming Forth By Day*. We know it as *The Book of the Dead*. I think it holds a lot that we, living in their future, can still use, providing its meaning, rites and symbols are brought into our own time and used in a manner appropriate to that time. We might give it a new title as well and call it *The Book of Living Forever*.

Ancient Fears

We may not be able to avoid physical death, but we can prepare for it while we still live, and take much of the fear, uncertainty, and apprehension out of it when the moment comes. Our Western culture tends to push away the thought of death, to relegate it to some unknown and indeterminate time in the future. In the East they tend to live with the idea of death as something that is always at one's elbow. Many Westerners put off making a will because they either consciously or subconsciously feel that once they have done it, death is just that bit nearer. The truth of it is that death can come at any time from birth onwards, regardless of whether or not you have made a will. There will always be a few rare souls who look upon death as the last great excitement. As James Barrie said in Peter Pan, ' . . . to die will be an awfully big adventure . . .'. For an Initiate of the Ancient Mysteries that is exactly what it should be: an adventure: a journey through unknown waters to a beckoning land beyond.

I think perhaps my own favourite vision of death as a journey for which only single tickets are available comes from

J.R.R. Tolkien's book *Lord of the Rings*. Frodo, having boarded one of the last Elven ships to leave the Grey Havens, sails off into the unknown, and:

> . . . at last on a night of rain Frodo smelled a sweet fragrance on the air and heard the sound of singing that came over the water . . .

That is how it should be for us as we step over the threshold between life and death. That is how it can be if we use the instructions handed down to us from ancient times for this, the last journey, and perhaps the most important of all.

The Qualities of Life and Death

We often speak about something we call the Quality of Life, and if that exists then there must also be a Quality of Death, for nothing in the universe has a meaning without having an opposite. Let us then look at these Qualities and try to define them. We have a good Quality of Life if we have all our senses, if we are strong in health and have a body that obeys our mental commands. We have Quality of Life if we have intelligence and can earn our living without being a burden on others, if we can have children, have a decent place in which to live and work, and when we have a sense of self respect. Is that all there is to it? What about those who are blind, or deaf, or both, the people whose bodies cannot obey their will. There are people who can never take a job, who do not have a nice house to live in, who cannot have the child they long for or who have had a child and have lost it. There are people without work whose feelings of worthiness and self respect have been lost. Have they then no Quality of Life? The answer is yes, they do, because Quality is not how much one has but how one uses what is available. People born without arms can and do paint; paraplegics drive cars; victims of Downs Syndrome can be helped to attain a great deal of self reliance; there are children waiting for adoptive parents to love them; and there are many people who have lost jobs and have gone on to do the things they have always wanted to do and made a success out of seeming failure. Quality is not found in 'the good life' as pictured in the glossy magazines but in achieving the best we can with what we have, utilizing our potential as far as we can and knowing our full worth as a human being. In short, taking to heart the instruction given to all students of the Mysteries: 'Know Thyself'.

The Quality of Death is very similar in that it may come swiftly and unexpectedly; it may take its time; it can be hard or gentle, welcomed or raged at, but come it will to each and every one of us. There is a right way to live our lives and equally there is a right way in which to die. If we allow it to do so, Death can come as a friend, a release, a dream, a burst of glory or it can be dreaded, feared, denied and resented. Its Quality can be enhanced by applied knowledge and it can, in some circumstances, become an Initiation process that bestrides both worlds. There is a time to fight for more life and a time to let go and let the night-shaded pinions lift us away from the outworn and no longer usable physical shell.

I was taught as a student of the Mysteries that it was the right of every Initiate to go over in full consciousness, but that

Figure 1.1 Dancing twin death gods, Tibet.

few choose to do this. I asked why, and was told that it took time, patience and courage, and even an Initiate was sometimes tempted to simply let things take its course. It was this more than anything else that has prompted me to write this book. Perhaps also because I am now in my sixties and will soon need to begin the preparations for my own last journey so that all is arranged and I can get on with those tasks that are still left for me to do.

In the last few years there have been many books on death. It seems that ancient memories of guiding the dying over the last few days of life are stirring once more. Many people who were once part of the Priesthoods of Anubis, Hermes, Persephone and the other Psychopompoi of the Ancient world, and whose work concerned the guidance of the dying and the dead, have returned to the physical level and to take up their old occupation. It is time to rewrite the old Rituals by which an Initiate of the Mysteries loosed the ties to this level and took the road into the West, to Amenti, or Annwn, or Elysium; any one of a hundred names by which we designate that most mysterious of destinations.

Modern Death Customs Pre 1940

The modern world, with its emphasis on haste, enjoyment at all costs, acquisition of goods, and getting to the top, leaves little or no time for people to contemplate their death even if they wished to do so. But to meditate upon death is what we must learn to do if we are to get the most out of the experience when it comes. Even up to the beginning of World War Two it was one of the greatest concerns of an elderly person that they should be buried properly and to this end most of them took out small insurances to cover their modest expectations of a decent funeral. As a young girl I can remember the old people talking about their 'send off' with a sense of occasion. 'I've enough put by to see me off properly' was the north country way of saying it. 'Enough' meant a good quality coffin, and a good turn out of friends and neighbours with 'a bit of a do afterwards' – this was usually sandwiches and beer for the men, with biscuits and cake and a glass of sherry for the women.

A funeral then was an event in the small communities that

flourished between the wars, along with births and marriages. It was a time when one supported a neighbour, went along to the church to sing, somewhat self-consciously, the hymns that had been carefully chosen by the deceased, and spoke well of the departed, forgetting past wrangles and the little disputes that sometimes raised their heads. More rarely, one was treated to a full-bodied male voice choir from the local colliery or factory, singing with the fervour and strength that seem to be so much a part of the heritage of the Welsh and the Northern Counties. Death held a simple dignity in those days; it was accepted as being a part of Life.

Nowadays, when the medical profession has pushed back the boundaries of death and added years of life to our expectancy there is a different attitude. Once the very old and the very ill were allowed to quietly drift towards the farthest shore, usually in their own homes and with their loved ones around them. Perhaps, if they were churchgoers, the Parish priest or one of their chosen denomination would also be there, and the time would be spent talking quietly among themselves, occasionally addressing a comforting word to the person lying so still in the bed. The sense of hearing, always the last to fade, was kept alive with the murmured words of those gathered around. This would have given a feeling of being loved and cherished right to the last moment. When at last all was over, the head of the family would go to the neighbours and friends waiting in the parlour or kitchen – perhaps if they were well liked there would even be a group waiting outside. 'Well,' they would say, 'it's over, he/she's gone, and made a good end.' Then the women would take over what has always been their work as the priestesses of both Birth and Death, The Preparation of the Dead. Sometimes the local midwife would also be the Layer Out; at other times the women of the family with a few friends would give this last service themselves. The body would be washed from head to foot, hair combed and arranged, nails cleaned, and laid out in its best clothes, or maybe an old-fashioned shroud bought years before and put aside until needed. The front parlour would be rearranged so that the coffin could be placed there, open, for friends and family to take a last look at their departed. When at last the hearse arrived women would come to their front doors to watch with silent sympathy. The gossip would be of how the dead had been seen by the local community; incidents and anecdotes would be swapped; tales of bygone events recalled and old differences forgotten for the most part. After the funeral, those invited would gather at the house to eat, drink and talk. Dress would be sober in colour, often the only time that particular suit, coat or dress would be worn. The air of slight gloom that hung over everyone was considered a fitting tribute to the dead. Within a few days life would go on and, although remembered, perhaps tearfully for a while, the one who has passed through the Gates would have been allowed to depart without let or hindrance.

How different it is today. Old people are, in many cases, taken from their much-cherished homes where they may have lived all their adult lives and where they feel safe, and instead placed in a home. Once there they may deteriorate rapidly because there is little or no mental or emotional stimulation. There are no real neighbours and often no family, or at least none near at hand. The old communities have gone, tower blocks have replaced small houses, strangers have replaced friends and neighbours.

When illness comes it is spent in an anonymous hospital bed with overworked and weary doctors and nurses trying to cope with the still living so that, although they do their best, the dying is often done alone. Gone is recognition of the occasion's dignity – the intent is to keep them breathing at all costs, including their own desire to leave. Death, which should come as a friend, often comes instead in the company of tubes and syringes, harsh lights, catheters and the noise and bustle of an overcrowded ward. In the past, Death was understood, its place in the scheme of things was known and provided for. Now it is seen as simply another barrier to push back and perhaps even to eliminate in time.

I should emphasize that we are talking here of those for whom Death has become inevitable either through age, illness or circumstance. There is indeed a time to fight for life, and fight one should, but equally there is a time to accept that this incarnation is drawing to its close.

Fear of Losing the Self

Why do so many fear death, even those who profess a deep belief in their particular religion? Listening to and watching

services of different denominations and faiths, I have noted
that all exhort their followers to a belief in a future life of joy
and peace and closeness with their Saviour, God or Prophet.
The Hereafter is proclaimed to be a 'better life', so why then
do so many fear what they are told lies ahead? It would appear
that though many may attend worship and try to live
according to the tenets of their faith, there are those among
them who cannot bring themselves to trust what they hear or
are told. For example, if one looks through the hymnbooks of
any Christian Sect, it may be seen that many of their words
implore the Almighty to make His followers poor, humble and
lowly. If those that sing the words so fervently returned home
to find that their wishes had been granted, recrimination
would most likely be the order of the day.

The answer to the question posed above seems, in almost
all cases, to be the fear of losing the Consciousness of the
present Self with all its attendant memories, experiences and
knowledge. Unless one understands how the spirit evolves,
this apparent eclipse of the Self can be hard to take.

Some people have a fanatical belief in their version of
Paradise, while others hold no hope at all and state that they
expect only an obliteration of consciousness and all that goes
to make one an individual. Some profess a belief that is three
parts hope and one part apprehension, a few turn that
estimate around and it becomes three parts apprehension and
one part hope. While there are many reputable mediums for
whom the truth is the highest Ideal, the money to be made
in providing such people with proof positive of survival has
long been a source of income to the unethical. If someone
came up with a costly but feasible invention that could
provide actual contact with the dead, they would be
oversubscribed within days. Literally billions would be
poured into it if it was thought it had a chance. The same
amount of money could probably turn the Sahara into the
lush, grass-filled land it was long ago.

Death in the Ancient World

How did the ancient world feel about Death, and what do the
Mystery Religions have to say on the subject? Did they fear
it as much as those in our time, or did they accept it with more

trust than their twentieth-century counterparts?

I think it would be true to say that humanity has always feared death to an extent, but in the times when the great Mediterranean cultures flourished the ordinary people expected less of life, were contented with less, accepted that life was short, much shorter than it is now, and held a simple faith that all would be well. Today much of the world is educated to an extent beyond the comprehension of our ancestors, and being educated brings with it a new and far greater fear of the unknown.

In the ancient priesthoods of Egypt and Greece, and those lands we now refer to as the Middle East, philosophers and great thinkers such as Anaxamander, Thales and Pythagoras, Socrates, Plato, Solon, Hypatia and others were among the most educated minds of their day. How then did they view death? Some had faith enough to treat it as a mere inconvenience, as with the death of Socrates who was calm and unhurried to the end. Others pondered it, talked about it, studied it, but apparently did not fear it.

Humanity at that time seemed closer to its Gods and to the beliefs concerning those Gods which naturally included the Death Rites. The inevitability of dying was something that, like the seasons, was experienced by everyone from priest to peasant, merchant to slave, king to beggar. One got on with one's life until it was time to die. It was that simple. Or was it?

The priesthood had a deeper insight into this unending circle of the two opposites. They saw all around them evidence that death was by no means the end, that sometimes seeming death was renewed in a cycle that went on and on. Their training in the subtle sciences of mind and spirit, a science that all but disappeared in the smoke of Alexandria, enabled them to understand more and to probe deeper into things that today are dismissed by scientists as being without foundation or proof, and denounced by Fundamentalists as being the work of the Devil. The truth is that the ancient priesthood of all lands practising a form of Mystery Religion held an unshakeable conviction that another, higher level of Being existed beyond our ability to see or reach whilst in the physical body.

The Raising of the God

The actual 'Mysteries' were, in point of fact, ritual Initiation dramas and in almost all cases were enactments of the death of the local God and his yearly resurrection. Enclosed within those same Mysteries, however, were Rites and Rituals dealing with other areas of life. There is little to distinguish between the way in which Christians celebrate Easter with the mourning of the Crucifixion of Jesus his death, burial and subsequent rising after three days in the tomb and the celebration of the Osirian and Eleusian Mysteries of the ancient world.

The ritual of Initiation followed a similar process especially in Egyptian Temples, where the neophyte, in order to undergo the experience of 'death in life', was often enclosed within a cave, which was then sealed, or inside a sarcophagus over which a heavy stone lid was placed. All this was a test of endurance and courage to make certain the new priest or priestess was worthy of the title of Initiate before being 'brought back to life' by the High Priest. It is for this reason that Initiates are often referred to as being 'Twice Born' or, as in the case of Melchisedek, described as having neither father nor mother and being without descent or, and this is significant, *end of days*. The Ritual was believed by the priesthood of those times to confer not immortality in the sense of living continuously, but the knowledge that the vital part of the human being went on after physical death.

The tradition of giving the soul time to separate from the physical is adhered to by many faiths. Even in our own time when everything is accomplished at speed, there is usually a three day lapse between death and burial of the body, and most Initiates stipulate this time lapse in their wills. This does not, however, happen in those countries where the day-time temperatures are such that an almost immediate disposal of the remains is a necessity, but it is generally held that it takes three days for the subtle body to completely separate from the rapidly decomposing physical form and become fully aware of its new self.

By joining the ranks of the Initiated it was believed that one would by-pass the rather dull world to which the ordinary run of humanity went after death. One went instead directly to the level of the Gods and lived with them, at least until it was time to return to a new life on the physical level. The general public, as it were, crossed the Styx, or stepped into the Death Barge steered by Anubis and set off for a place that was virtually the same as the one they had left, with the exception that there was no hunger, no disease, and no worry.

The awe-inspiring spectacle of entry into the Mysteries both in Greece and Egypt were often great public occasions which were seen as a means of impressing the populace. The actual testing of the candidate would have taken place over a period of time, maybe months, weeks or days before the actual Ritual of Initiation itself. However the splendour and ceremony that accompanied the conferring of the priesthood upon the new priest or priestess gave the people an excuse for a holiday and a feast, while allowing them at the same time to witness the power of the priesthood.

Primitive Beliefs

It would seem that there has never been a time when humanity did not believe in a life, or at least some form of existence, after death. The most primitive races as far back as we can discover have always buried their dead, placed them beneath the floors of their cave dwellings, or just covered them with stones, along with possessions, trinkets, clay pots and perhaps a little dried meat or grain. Clearly they believed they would in some way continue to exist. The word 'exist' gives us a clue to one of humanity's greatest fears concerning death which is, will we still exist in a form we can recognize as ourselves? Will we still be able to say, 'I', and know that 'I' to be the personality we were in life? It is the obliteration of self memory, the loss of the 'I' that appears to worry people most.

Among the early primitive races dreams and the memory of dreams were a very real thing. To them a dream occurred in a real place with real people, and who is to say they were wrong. They felt that if they dreamed of a dead relative or friend it proved that they still existed, somewhere. That somewhere became, over long periods of time, the dwelling places of the dead: Amenti; Elysium; Hades; The Summerlands, etc. In those dreams the dead were alive, looking as they had always looked; sometimes they even gave messages, warnings, or advice. In this way early man

Figure 1.2 God of Death, Maya.

gradually built up an idea of what he expected to find after physical death had claimed him.

With life at that time so hard and unrelenting, so full of danger, hunger, pain and fear, is it any wonder that the afterlife was pictured as being easier, needing nothing to make it a pleasant existence? A place where food animals were plentiful, where edible roots, grains and berries grew close to hand, a place where one could hunt but never get killed, where disease was unknown and pain something that had been left far behind. Still, it was the actual dying that was so frightening, especially when it involved injury, pain and terror. At that time humanity began to reach deep within to seek out the inner flame of the spirit and, in so doing, took on the first and greatest of all Quests: the search for the Higher Self.

The Priesthood of Anubis

In the times of dynastic Egypt, death was seen as something to be anticipated, almost desired. The work of the Priesthood of Anubis was concerned with easing the physical side of dying and guiding the soul as it slowly separated itself from the body. Anubis and his Greek and Roman counterparts Mercury and Hermes were all given the title 'Psychopompos', the Guide of the Dead. Both God forms were seen as Messengers of the High Gods, and were considered to be the sons of the Father God, or the main male figure of that particular Pantheon. Anubis was the son of Osiris and his sister Nephthys, Hermes the son of Zeus by the nymph Maia, and Mercury the son of Jove or Jupiter by a nymph. In later times the Greek Hermes and the Egyptian Anubis became joined to become a single entity referred to as Hermanubis.

It is significant that both Hermes and Anubis, besides being conductors of the dead, were also considered to be great Teachers of Humanity, and indeed so too is Death a great teacher. We can see a similar method of symbolism in the figure of Saturn not only as a form of the Grim Reaper, but also as The Disciplinarian or Teacher. The earliest form of Saturn is that of a bearded woman, a symbol that can reveal a great deal of power when meditated upon. The meaning becomes clearer when one realizes that it is the female who should be seen as the Death God/dess, as in the Sumerian

Figure 1.3 Anubis, Lord of the Necropolis.

Pantheon where Ereshgigal rules the Underworld of the Dead. It is Woman who is Alpha and Omega, the Beginning and the End, for who else gives birth into Life, and in doing so pronounces the sentence of death upon the child she births.

At the time of the Mystery Religions what happened after death dependeded on how one's life had been lived, as indeed most modern religions aver today. In Egypt, passing the scrutiny of the Forty Two Assessors meant answering their questions concerning one's life and actions, a daunting task when you read those questions slowly and carefully. They are as relevant today as they were 4,000 years ago. *The Book of the Dead* was designed to give careful and implicit instructions on how to deal with every part of the journey between physical death and the welcome entry into the land of Amenti.

The promise of Hellfire and eternal Damnation spent languishing in mental terror and physical agony by those sinning against the Laws laid down by the Church only really became part of the Afterlife when Christianity swept into power. It promised, so the common people thought, immortality within the physical life and thousands entered this new religion which promised such a prize. As proof of this the story of the Raising of Lazarus was told and retold. The fact that it was almost a word for word, action for action description of a Ritual Initiation into a Mystery School was not realized at the time because this was knowledge given only to those preparing to take entry into the priesthood.

Death in the Modern World

How does the modern Initiate deal with all this? We live in an era full of wonder as well as danger and crisis and those who walk the Path of the Mysteries today must look upon themselves as both Guardians of an incredibly ancient Knowledge system, and as Warriors fighting for a planet that is on the verge of being overwhelmed by greed and the desire for power. Yet in the midst of this terrifying scenario for a possible Armageddon such a one must also try to find a point of serenity within where that inevitable meeting with Thanatos[1] may be prepared for and acknowledged as an inescapable fact. We are groomed by our parents, family and teachers when we are young for the adult life that lies ahead. We go to school, college and maybe university to learn how to deal with the technologies of our modern era, yet few, if any, know how to extend that preparation to include death and what lies beyond, even though it is a logical progression of thought.

The students of a modern Mystery School begin with a disadvantage. Unlike their ancient counterparts their desire for study and knowledge is at best dismissed by the establishment as being of little importance, and at worst denounced as heretical, satanic, anti-Christian and dangerous to the well being of 'God fearing Christians'. (I stop to ask myself why one should be exhorted to fear a Being described as a God of Love.) There are no proud and graceful Temples open to all faiths and traditions, offering teaching in the old ways and dignified and awe-inspiring Initiation ceremonies. We must teach in quiet and silent ways, offering the ancient knowledge only to the determined and dedicated few who seek us out. Initiations are still offered but not with the openness and joy we would like.

But still the Flame of Knowledge survives and is passed from hand to hand, and among those teachings we can still find the one which shows the way to Amenti. This teaching has many names: 'The Way of the Soul to the Light', 'The Way of the Jackal' and 'The Dance of the Butterfly' are examples.

The Symbol of the Butterfly

The use of the Butterfly as a symbol for the soul is more than chance, it is a direct indication of survival. Consider the life cycle of this insect. It is born from the gene pool of its species. It lives in the form of a caterpillar; a form in which it simply eats, sleeps, and grows. If it escapes the maw of a hungry bird it will eventually seek out a quiet place and begin to spin itself a cocoon. In doing so it obeys an age-old Law by which all butterflies are bound to life. Once settled within its tiny coffin, it begins to die, but only in the form it has worn until that moment. But it is still, in a sense, a caterpillar. Nothing has been added, nothing has been taken away, the silken web enclosing it is merely a protection during its change from one level of existence to another. The cocoon is, in fact, a sarcophagus.

Within its tiny shroud a miracle will take place. What was once the body of a caterpillar will rot down and return to its basic constituents and *reform* into a completely new shape. It will have a new body with new appetites, a new way of living, and it will have become a creature of air rather than of earth. At the appointed time the 'tomb of Initiation' breaks open and from it emerges a form of winged beauty. Can anything be more different from what went before? Yet this ethereal creature with such delicate wings and body has been formed out of exactly the same set of molecules, the same genetic material, as the actual body of the caterpillar. This new form will seek out a mate and ensure the survival of its species and its own individual characteristics before undergoing a second death and, maybe, changing again.

As human beings, gifted with the power of thought, imagination, creativity and a physical form designed to make use of them, plus the touch of genius that enables us to store experience in the form of memory, can we think ourselves less than the humble caterpillar? Would we be given all this only to be a fleeting life, to live for only a short while in the sun before going down forever into the dark? Such a waste would make a mockery of the wonder and beauty of the universe in which nothing is lost forever, but remains caught in the vibrations that continually reverberate through the cosmos. We too spend time like a caterpillar, eating and learning and growing, then we seek out a place in which to begin our great Change. Unlike the insect we spend a lot of our time worrying about this change: whether it will hurt; whether it will go according to plan; and whether we will remember being as we were. The caterpillar does not worry about remembering what it was like to crawl around eating leaves: it knew it was a caterpillar then; it knows it is a butterfly now; that is what is important in such a tiny life.

Reincarnation

Very few people can remember what it was like the last time they walked the earth, and those who can, remember only in fragments like a broken cine film in black and white. The passion and the drama, the pain and the joy are no longer white hot, but far off dreams of themselves. Only when the links with the physical are broken can full memory be recovered, for to remember fully whilst living a different life with different loves would be too traumatic for the soul to accept.

Joan Grant once said in describing reincarnation that it was like a necklace, each separate bead was a separate life with a separate personality, but that which animated all the lives and bound them together was the spirit, the Oversoul if you prefer, which she saw as the thread running through the centre of each bead binding them all together into one circle of experience. It is a very good analogy but I have my own variation on this, one that stems from my training in the theatre. Every actor or actress during their time on the stage plays many parts. Some will be contemporary, others will be costume drama, some will be tragic parts and yet others will be full of laughter. At the end of their careers old actors and actresses like to sit and reminisce about those parts. They will remember bits and pieces of the words they spoke, the costumes they wore, and those with whom they worked. We are like actors playing out many parts within the destined circle of lives allotted to us for our cosmic education. Each part is a life, the personality of that time, the actor himself is the thread running through those parts binding them all together. It is the *real* person, the actor, not the character that incarnates.

Let us look at a third analogy. Open your wardrobe and look at the coats, dresses, suits, etc. hanging there. Each one is on a hanger and the hangers are joined by the rod that runs the length of the wardrobe. Consider each of those garments to be one life lived, its colour, style, and condition indicative of the incumbent personality. The important thing is the rod that links them: it alone touches all of them, combines them, supports them and knows each one intimately. The trained Initiate learns to walk up and down the corridors of time symbolized by the wardrobe, lightly touching each garment and smiling at the fleeting touch of memory.

An Initiate's Preparation for Death

Initiates prepare for life and for death because they know they are two sides of the same coin, that one without the other is unthinkable and unknowable. Perfect trust and perfect love is the way that one Tradition puts it. We have been born and have died many times before and will do so again. That is easy to say, not easy to prove, not something that is easy to teach. In my book *The Sacred Cord Meditations*,[1] I have given instructions on coping with one's memories of death and how to search them out and deal with them in a way that lessens the impact.

It is neither morbid nor premature to consider the possibility of death even if one is young and healthy. We live in an age when, despite the advances in medicine and the lengthening of life expectancy, sudden death is never very far from us. It must not be pushed into the background of our lives to lurk there like some spectre but looked at with clear eyes and a calm heart. The whole object of this book is to show those who tread the Way of the Mysteries how they can open the way for themselves and be able to look Death in the face and be unafraid.

I have a friend who, in his teenage years, experienced a series of ongoing dreams in which he travelled to some place like an inland sea. In the distance he could see an island, and moored close to where he stood was a small boat. The figure of Death, his face covered by the hood of his cloak, sat near by. He was there, so he told the dreamer, to be ready to ferry across to the island those who had left the earth sphere. In his dreams he saw Death as a rather lonely person with no one to share his solitude. So he sat and talked with him.

A few dreams later Death invited him to visit his home. On arrival my friend found that Death had a daughter younger than himself who was badly crippled. This was a source of great sorrow to Death who loved her dearly. The dream sequences unfolded slowly over a period of many months during which he visited both Death, and Death's daughter to talk to her and keep her company when her father was away. Moved by a sudden impulse he gave her on one occasion an oboulos, a coin or token traditionally placed in the hand of the dead in ancient times to pay their way over the Styx.

In the last dream of this kind he found the house empty. He found only Death who told him that his daughter had died that day and he had taken her across to the island. He thanked him for giving her the coin and for being her companion, and promised him that when the time came for his own death, he would come gently and as a friend. Then, for the first time he showed him his face.

This series of dreams was quite spontaneous and took place over a fairly long period of time: almost a year. But it shows that an interaction with the symbol/idea of Death as a personality can be built. The unusual part of these dreams was the fact that Death's daughter was mortal and subject to her father's visitation, even having to pay for her crossing over the waters. Death remains a mystery it seems even to those closest to it. We must accept that and prepare for it.

1 Thanatos, the Greek God of Death.
2 *The Sacred Cord Meditations*, Aquarian Press 1990, page 45.

2

The Other Side of Life

To see a world in a grain of sand,
and a Heaven in a wild flower,
Hold Infinity in the palm of your hand.
And Eternity in an hour . . .
William Blake, 1757–1827

Death in Old Age

Three score years and ten is the biblical reckoning for a human life time, but many of the great men and women of the past have lived far longer than that and modern science has pushed the boundaries of death back even further. It is not uncommon for both men and women to live well into their eighties, and the science of gerontology has become well established. It has also been discovered that long life runs in families, so there is reason to suppose that longevity is, to some degree at least, genetic. My own family on both sides tends to live well into the late eighties and even nineties with the added bonus of both mental and physical well being right up to the time of death. (This piece of personal information may not be welcomed by everybody!)

Long life does not always equate with mental alertness, however, and many elders slide into a childish state of mind which acts as a gentle anaesthesia as the physical body approaches the end of its existence. In many cases this can be prevented or at least kept at bay by keeping the mind active and the spirit filled with a sense of adventure and wonder right up to the last moment. We might give as an example Queen Eleanor of Aquitaine, the wife of Henry the second of

England. Eleanor was for her time an exceptionally long lived woman surviving well into her eighties. In an era when women were expected to bear a child every year, to say nothing of the risk of plague, bad food and the ever present threat of war, this was not far short of being miraculous. She was a very special woman: the wife of two kings and the mother of two more, plus several daughters who became queen's consorts. She accompanied her first husband, Louis of France, to the Crusades, riding alongside him daringly dressed in men's clothing. She survived the twin scandals of adultery and divorce, and the trauma of being shut up in a Tower for many years by her second husband. Eleanor was a fighter, a survivor, and a woman who kept both her head and her sense of humour and who was not afraid to take risks, at any age. She was, moreover, among those responsible for the emergence of the celebrated Courts of Love and the Age of the Troubadours.

The intrigue and battles that had beset her life increased as she got older. At an age when most women even today have retired to look after their gardens and grandchildren, she was scouring England for money to pay Richard the Lionheart's ransom. She lived through the deaths, probably murders, of her second son Geoffrey and her grandson Arthur of Brittany and saw her youngest son John come to the throne of England only to lose most of the French lands belonging to the English Crown, including her own vast Duchy of Aquitaine. The only surviving part of the once vast possessions is the Channel Islands.

The need for a constant state of mental alertness was very probably the impetus that kept Eleanor going. It is a proven fact that as long as elderly people are given access to ongoing mental stimulus and feel that they have a part to play in their family and community, they will retain a state of mental alertness. They certainly have a greater chance than those condemned to a life of mere existence from one meal to the next, the only excitement being a dutiful visit from relatives, maybe once a week. Although there are undoubtedly times when it becomes impossible for the family to look after an elderly relative, it is always better for them if they can stay where they can feel they are still part of the family unit. Having said that, not all elderly people are sweet and gentle and easy to look after, some of them can be extremely trying, obstinate, and even, let it be whispered, downright cantankerous.

Honouring the Elders

In some countries the status of the older age group is one of honour and the younger members are taught to look up to them for their accumulation of wisdom and knowledge. It is they who provide the all important links between the past, present and future, as symbolized by their grandchildren and great-grandchildren. Japan nominates many of its older people, those who have a particular skill that they actively hand on to the next generation, as National Treasures, a title that must make them feel that they still have worth in the eyes of their friends and family.

The Gentle Voyage

Death, when it comes to the elderly, should be seen as a gentle voyage home, a reward for a life well lived and experience undergone with fortitude. It is important that they are not made to feel either a burden or a nuisance but gathered into the family so the last weeks and days may be spent together quietly and with love. This is even more important when the person concerned is, in esoteric terms, unaware, for theirs is the greater need for comfort, companionship, and a reassurance that they will not be forgotten by those they are leaving behind. To be forgotten is a frightening thing for them, more so than death itself for it feels like obliteration in a very real sense. I have said in *The Sacred Cord Meditations* that there are three Truths we must all face:

1   You will grow old, everyone does, though it may seem to the very young that it will never happen to them.
2   Those things that have given you such pleasure, that you have collected and treasured throughout your life must be given up, for you can take nothing with you when you go.
3   You will in time be forgotten, as immortal fame is given to only a few.
    But you will live on in your descendants and family.

But during the process of dying, it is important that the elderly are reassured that during your time at least they will be remembered with love.

Helping Them to Pass Over

The practice of naming a child after grandparents is seldom seen in modern times except in families that have a long tradition of certain names. But there is no doubt that even if it is given as a second or third name the older person sees it as something far beyond a mere compliment, it is a promise that part of them will go on. A forename is a deeply personal thing, indeed in esoteric circles one's given name is considered to be truly magical and to hold a meaning and purpose. In other cultures it is the practice to be given two names, one to be known and used, the other to hold as a secret and a source of power.

It is, therefore, of great importance to an elderly person nearing the end of their time on earth to be called by their given name instead of simply Mum, Mother, or Grandma, Dad, or Grandfather. If they have already lost their life partner then it is even more important because they will not have heard their personal name used for a long time, unless by a contemporary or a still living sister or brother. It gives a tremendous lift to hear one's name called in the voice of someone known and loved. A little thing, but very important. They may towards the end enjoy listening to favourites pieces of music, or looking at old photos of family and friends. Sometimes they may just want to sit or lie quietly with someone holding their hand.

Special Needs and Worries

For those who are 'aware', death is seen in a different light. If the ending is gradual then plans can be made and talked over with family, friends, or Temple brethren. The procedure for burial and the Rites that will accompany it can be discussed and invocations, prayers, hymns or chants can be chosen. It is also a time to actually give away things and have the fun of seeing people's faces light up.

People need company when they are dying, unless they demand to be left alone. They need to talk to friends and to family, to explain things, to go over past experiences sometimes time and time again. They may need to say sorry for things they have said or done in the past, or to seek reassurance or a promise that certain things will be done in the future. Often they worry about their pets being left without anyone to care for them, or a treasured plant being left to wither. These things are important to them at this time, they should be listened to and given assurances that all will be well.

An elderly Initiate may wish to have some time alone in order to prepare and perhaps to summon those they wish to see as they open their eyes on a different world. They may ask for certain people to come and see them, or to perform certain short rituals to open the Gates. In a hospital this can be difficult, but a sympathetic Ward Sister can sometimes be persuaded to put the screens around a bed to give some privacy. Above all they will need someone to keep going over their 'Death Pathworking'[1] with them. If an around the clock attendance is not possible, see that the working is recorded so that they can listen to it either with earphones or with the volume turned low. Instructions for this kind of pathworking are given in a later chapter.

There are all too few trained people working along esoteric lines who take on the modern version of the Priesthood of Anubis. They visit anyone whose family may not be able, or even willing to come every day and take on the role of Lodge Brother or Sister. This is specialized work and should only be undertaken after training has been given that will enable the 'priest' or 'priestess' to help both the aware and the unaware, as required by their work. If an untrained person attempts this they can do more harm than good and may antagonize the family and upset the patient. The main concern is to make the departure one of grace and dignity so the elder feels cherished and loved as they pass through the Gates.

Death in the Young

If death in the elderly with a full life behind them can be seen as a completeness of that life. Death in the young is tragic and heartrending. The life has barely begun and seemed to hold so much promise for the child and its family. To have that promise snatched away is one of life's greatest traumas. With the elderly, death comes mostly as a result of old age, of the decline in the body's defences against disease, shock and pneumonia following a fall or an accident. In the young there are other causes and some of them bring the extra burden of self-inflicted guilt, the feeling of 'If only I had . . . or had not . . .' or sometimes the even more devastating realization that a beloved child has gone beyond one's reach without even

Figure 2.1

time to say goodbye. This is most often seen in the case of traffic accidents, violent crimes against children, or disasters that could not have been foreseen but which add inevitably to the grief suffered by the parents and family of the child who has gone on.

Many years ago, on the continent, there was a tragically large loss of life when a circus tent caught fire. The greater part of the dead were children and in many cases entire families of children were lost leaving the parents with totally ruined and empty lives. For one mother the loss was made the more bitter because she had scolded her young son before he left over some small misdemeanour and had refused to kiss him goodbye. His subsequent death she saw as a personal punishment and refused to see it in any other way, eventually ending her own life.

Unfortunately far too many children die as the result of careless driving, sometimes with a parent at the wheel of the car. Others are the victims of hit and run. Caution and road sense are things we all try to instil into our children, and the day we let a son or daughter out alone on their first bicycle is filled with dread. But unless we want to tie them to us hand and foot and, in doing so, stifle their natural instincts to fly the nest, we must learn to let them go, to try their wings and trust that we have taught them well enough. Too many are given bikes but not sent to the training classes held by the Police Force in many towns. How many children are not just sent to swimming lessons, but actively encouraged to take life-saving classes as well.

We all tell our children not to take anything from a stranger, not to get into a car with one, but is it enough? A child's greatest fear is being separated from its parents, so a stranger in a car saying, 'Your mummy has been in an accident. You are to go to the hospital with me', is playing on that fear with terrible consequences. It is far better to tell the child not to believe anything that may be said, and risk the story being true than to subject the child to rape, violence or even death. An even better idea is to give the child a password by which it may know for certain that the summons comes from you.

Sharing the Grief

Death also comes in more silent ways, through birth defects and cot deaths, through disease and inherited disorders. The parting is no less hard to bear, but there is the blessing of being able to guide the child through the actual process of death, of being able to hold it and soothe it through those long dark hours. The burden falls heavily upon the mother who gave the child physical birth, but do not underestimate the grief felt by the father whose seed began the process of life. Our society is one that frowns on men giving vent to their grief in the form of tears, but here the strength of the woman can prevail and she should encourage her partner to fully express his pain. It is of the utmost importance that both parents express their grief to each other, then they will have the strength to help their child through the process of death. It is often the child who helps the parents for they, already close to the borderline between life and death, have an instinctive knowledge of how to accomplish the passing.

Murder and Violent Death

With violent crime on the increase in the major cities of the world, death at the hands of another person, in short, murder, is something that must be counted as a possibility. The average man and woman may think that such an end is for 'others', never for them, never for ordinary folk, but those who suffer murder are for the most part ordinary people themselves, who did not expect their ending to come in this manner, who also thought it only happened to 'others'.

The manner of dying concerns us all, no one likes to think of dying in a plane crash or being in a train wreck; most people would much rather die than live hopelessly crippled and deformed. We do not know, we can only surmise that at such a moment the psyche leaps free of the body. It is not given to us to know the hour of our departure or the manner in which it will come, but we can do our best to ensure that we are as ready as a human being ever can be to let go of the physical body when the time comes.

To pass over in such a way is traumatic for the psyche and it needs a great deal of help from both the living and those

Figure 2.2 God of Death, Aztec.

who work on the other side of life. This is especially true of children who die as a result of murder and violence. There is no time to ease the passing and often there is a considerable lapse of time before the results of the crime are discovered. This again puts enormous pressure upon those waiting for news and it is the living in such cases who suffer most and who need care and help. The victims have already passed beyond and are safe.

We should also look towards an understanding of the sacrificial death. This applies not simply to someone who, for instance, leaps in front of a train to save another person and dies in their stead, but also to those who die in battle, for this must also be counted as a sacrificial death. They may indeed go to war obeying the orders of their commanders, but they go also to defend a principle. Sometimes they may not entirely agree with that principle, but they obey, and in doing so they take on the possibility of sacrificial death.

The Willing Sacrifice

To die a willing victim means to die with great power as the Saviours down through the aeons have done, but the soldier, airman or sailor who dies in battle because that is the job he must do, is equally offering up a life for a life or lives. It does not matter which side he is on, if he dies for what he truly believes in then it is enough. Now we come to a dichotomy; if the soldier who dies in battle dies a sacrificial death at the hands of a soldier on the other side, what does that make the second soldier? Is he the murderer of a hapless victim, or is he also in his turn, if killed, a sacrifice?

From an esoteric point of view based on personal opinion, and it can only be personal and should not be considered a 'teaching', if the victim is to be considered as a sacrifice offered to save others, then he who kills cannot be seen as anything less than the sacrificial priest of old, even as Abraham would have sacrificed his only son in obedience to the Will of God. He too is obeying an order and defending a principle. The Commander who gives the order to advance, the mother who waves her son off to war, fearfully, but allowing him his choice, are both, in a sense, offering the life of another as a sacrifice for the good of others. Mary made the same choice in standing at the foot of the Cross. This, no matter how high sounding, offers little comfort to the mother mourning her son, or the wife her husband and the father of her children. It does not matter how much we may deplore war, there will always be times when we have to make a choice, to fight for a deeply held principle or give in and go under. Words solve little because they can be broken; actions, on the other hand, cause effects that, like a stone thrown into a pool, ripple on down the years.

Every death diminishes the world just as every birth enriches it, and this in itself is an eternal circle of entering and departing, of spring and winter, sowing and harvesting. In the Hindu beliefs, every single life on earth is a manifestation of the Creator, and in order to exist in the physical world it must feed upon itself, literally. Thus everything is sacrificed to everything else in order that the eternal wheel of life may revolve and evolve. In this we may perhaps see one meaning of the 'Lamb slain from the beginning of the world', for many of the Saviours have given their bodies to be eaten by their followers, usually in the symbolic sense only. But the myth of the dismemberment of the God is too widespread to ignore.

'Take and eat this, all of you for this is my Body.' The communion offers up bread and wine that in the act of transubstantiation become the actual flesh and blood of a Human God. This offering of the total Self, body and soul in order that a Great Mystery may unfold, has been sacred in many traditions and has been performed by many different Saviours. But, the offer made by a willing victim must be completed by a separate sacrificial act made by the one called upon to be the sacrificing agent. Thus it becomes an act complete in itself and death, instead of a defeat, becomes a triumph.

Let us now return to a point already made: that every woman, in giving birth, gives both life and death in one and the same moment, making a very clear reason for why Saturn can be none other than Female. It is She who continually offers her children to Death that they might live continually. It may well be that the legend of Lillith, condemned by the God of the Old Testament to give birth to thousands of children each day, and to see a third of them die in that same instant, has a deeper meaning than theologians and mythographers have yet understood. The late Alan Watts, one of the most notable writers in this field, said in *Myth and Christianity*:[2]

Physical death is then understood as the instrument of eternal renewal. It is not only the transformation of life into food; it is also the wiping away of memory, of the past, which, if it continued to accumulate indefinitely, would strangle all creative life with a sense of unutterable monotony. Physical death is the involuntary end of the memory-system called myself – the end of my time. But the real and eternal Self does not die at death – for the paradoxical reason that it wills to 'die', to 'end', eternally and is therefore 'new' at every moment . . . To put it less symbolically – the world of reality is ever present, always at an end because it has no future, and always new because it has no past.

Death as the True Mystery

Death is a true mystery, for nothing is known of it except its result. Birth, on the other hand, offers (hopefully) a lifetime of ongoing experience. If Death is a Birth into a new dimensional existence, then Birth must be a Death into a similar dimension, our own. All things follow on one from another, nothing can really end for the universe does not allow it. It allows change, but not annihilation; it gives rest, but does not remain static. If this is so for a universe, it must be so for humanity for we are an inescapable part of the universe. Without us, *it* cannot be complete, just as we cannot *be* without *it*.

In the world of the Initiate, therefore, Death is merely a junction where one gets off one train and onto another bound in a different direction rather than at a terminus where everything stops. Because such a one knows about and understands the complete oneness of the universe and everything within it, they also know that they can never be apart from those they love. Each new existence brings one into contact with both new and old loved ones and gradually the whole universe becomes aware of loving and being loved, evolving towards the ultimate goal which is the bringing together of the separate pieces of Life into one complete Whole. It is this desire for Wholeness that stands behind the many Dismemberment of the God myths. Without Death, change would not be noticed or even acknowledged, yet it is part of the necessary scheme of growth.

Suicide

We have not yet looked at another form of death which needs to be seen in the light of compassion and understanding, rather than condemnation: the matter of suicide, a deliberate act of self destruction in a fit of temper, fear, rage, pique or hysteria. The ending of a life that has become unbearable through pain and/or the mental agony of knowing one has become an intolerable burden on a much loved wife, husband, parent or child. The matter of choice, if one is trapped within a burning building, of jumping to death below, or burning. If one jumps, one is technically committing suicide, if one stays and does not take the million to one chance of surviving the jump, one is still committing suicide. What about the person who wakes up in the night and, thinking they have not taken their prescribed pills, takes more and overdoses.

Can they be accused of taking their own life?

We might also say of a soldier who, in order to save the lives of his comrades, goes against the enemy single-handed knowing full well that he will die, that he is deliberately throwing away his life, even if it is to save others. We have already looked at this kind of death and seen it as that of a willing sacrifice. But . . . is a willing sacrifice a suicide? It is all too easy to say, as many will indeed say, 'Oh, but that was different'. We might ask ourselves a question that is virtually impossible to answer: should Jesus have tried to save Himself from the sacrificial death on the Cross. The purists will say, 'But it had to be so to fulfil the prophesy', but the fact remains that if He chose not to save Himself, he was dying deliberately and with intent to die.

It is all too easy to follow the crowd and condemn, but unless we know all the details that may have led a human being to that dread decision we have no right to speak. That the Scales of Life must be adjusted goes without saying, but there must always be understanding and mercy in such cases, the souls have a special need once they have gone over, and they can and should be helped from our side of life.

We have spoken of the death by a violent act of one person against another, and I would like to suggest the reading of a small but important book by C.S. Lewis called *The Great Divorce*.[3] One of its characters, a mother whose son had been murdered, is met on the other side not by her son, but by his murderer. She cannot understand the point that is being made by this meeting and becomes hysterical and angry. The soul who has come to meet her points out that he is here because her son forgave him, can she do less? The son, because of his ability to forgive and love his murderer, has gone on to a higher level and sent instead his murderer to meet his mother. She, however, is unable to forgive and goes on suffering her loss over and over again. The book is well worth putting on your booklist for future reference as it contains much that is of interest to anyone intent on studying the other side of life.

Death is full of surprises and no one can take the ending of life, its circumstances, location or method for granted. The true Initiate understands this and makes plans accordingly as far as they can be made. By trying to understand what may be asked of the psyche at the moment of death we can make the moment less disturbing both for ourselves and for those we love. If a terminal illness allows us the time we can make the passing a higher Initiation taken in full consciousness and with love.

1 See *Highways of the Mind* by Dolores Ashcroft-Nowicki. Published by Aquarian Press, 1987.
2 *Myth and Christianity* by Alan Watts. Published by Thames & Hudson, 1983.
3 *The Great Divorce* by C.S. Lewis. Published by Fount, 1971.

3

Searching for Belief

Tis the sublime of man,
Our noontide Majesty, to know ourselves
Parts and proportions of one wondrous whole!
Samuel Taylor Coleridge, 1772–1834

Death and Religion

Different religions and beliefs direct the way we perceive the mystery of death. They may dictate how we come to the end and what we may decide has to be done with our remains afterwards. In the Christian faith this may mean asking for the presence of a priest at the end, for the comfort he may be able to offer both the dying and the family, for his prayers if this has been an integral part of the soul's human life, or for the rites of the church that they may be applied. Because of our religious history the West sees death in an entirely different way to that of other faiths and cultures. It has been said that we see it as an event that will give us either great joy or great suffering, but nothing in between.

Christianity would appear to offer little more than a continuous state of anxiety with regard to Death and the Afterlife. *If* you have led a good life, *if* you have not gone against the Commandments or the strictures of the Church, *if* you are truly worthy, then you will be spared damnation and be saved. But who is to say what is worthy, and have you been worthy *enough*? The point is that no one, and this includes the Church from the highest of its authorities to the lowest, really knows what will happen after Death. We can surmise, we can attempt to peer behind the veil and discuss near death experiences, and consult mediums by the score, but we will not know for sure until it is our turn, though we can make some guesses and prepare ourselves.

The Church of England and the Roman Catholic Church

The Church of England has set prayers for the dying and for immediately after death itself, but has little else to offer. The Roman Catholic Church has what are called 'The Last Rites', which contain Confession, Communion, and Unction. When the end is in sight, a priest is summoned to bring the Viaticum; he takes a Host from the ciborium (the cup that holds the Sacrament) and places it in a container called a Pyx. This is then veiled and taken to the house with bell and candle going before it. After some simple preparations and the donning of a purple stole the priest, alone with the dying person, hears their Last Confession and gives Absolution. Now and only now is the Host taken from the Pyx and the Communion offered and taken. This is followed by the Rite of Extreme Unction. The priest uses words and gestures laid down and used for hundreds of years, making the sign of the cross three times over the patient, and follows this by anointing the departing soul using the Oleum Infirmorum, a healing oil blessed and made sacred by the bishop. With it he seals the body on the eyes, ears, nose, mouth, hands, feet and thighs.

Thus cleansed of sin, both real and imagined, and feeling enclosed within the Rituals of their Church, the dying can feel safe and secure in the hope that they can go directly to Heaven, although they will still have to go before the Judgement Seat and may yet be sent to Purgatory for a greater or lesser time. Those left behind may pay to have Masses said for the departed soul and it is held that these will mitigate the punishment. Then, of course, there are Indulgences, and in earlier times these could be bought, so that a rich man could buy absolution but a poor man went in terror of Hell Fire.

Judaism

In Judaism there are no sacramental rites or ceremonies for the dying. Those around them invite them to speak and unburden themselves of any sin they may have committed. If unable to speak the dying person is asked to speak of them silently and in the heart. There is no anointing or washing of the dying person for it is unlawful to interfere with the dead or dying in any way. There is a solemn and beautiful prayer recited over the dying which is as follows:

> I acknowledge, O lord my God and God of my fathers, that my healing and my death are in Your hands. May it be Your will that you heal me with a perfect healing. But if I die may my death be an atonement for all the sins, transgressions, and iniquities which I have committed before You. Grant me my portion in the Garden of Eden, and let me attain the World to Come which is destined for the righteous.

It is considered a duty for someone to always be with the dying so that they do not die alone. When death is seen to be happening, those in the room, if they are Orthodox Jews, will tear their clothes, saying, 'Blessed be the truthful judge'.

Any water is then poured out of its containers, for death contaminates it. Death is traditionally confirmed by the cessation of the breath, and a feather or a mirror is held to the lips. Burial is as soon as possible. The body is sometimes anointed with spices at this time, and the Ashkenazi Jews smear the head, (the point at which the soul emerges and which is held sacred by so many different traditions) with a raw egg mixed with wine.

In Judaism, mourning follows a strict pattern in which certain foods and wine are forbidden. The time of mourning will depend on how closely related one is to the deceased. One mourns longer for a parent than for anyone else. The mourners may not cut their hair, shave, or wear certain things. Their shirts/coats are left torn. The funeral arrangements for a Jewish burial need different requirements, but modern Funeral Directors are well trained and know exactly what is needed and what they, as non-Jews, may or may not do. It is the same for other religions in our multi-racial society, where there is always advice and help at hand.

The Kaddish are prayers that praise God and petition for a

good life and peace in that life. They are *not* prayers of mourning but show that those who mourn are ready and willing to accept the will of God in all things. Kaddish will continue to be said for a whole year if the dead are one's parents, and always on the anniversary of their passing. The respect and love of the Jews for the elders of their family are part of their continual strength.

Looking Back Through Life

It is not always egotism that makes people write their life stories; eighty per cent perhaps, with another ten per cent writing them because they genuinely have something to record. Maybe another five write them as a form of revenge! There are, however, a small number who write them in answer to a subconscious urging to look back over their lives and seek a pattern.

An important part of occult training is the nightly review of the day's events in reverse order. It need not be in fine detail, just a broad outline will do, but it has a definite reasoning behind it. By going over the experiences of the day one can often see where a mistake has been made, where something that was said, or an action taken might have caused unintentional hurt or even actual harm to another person. Indeed, the intention to hurt may well have been there. By going over the events in the quietness preceding sleep one can often see more clearly how confrontation could have been avoided, how a situation could have been handled better, maybe even how an unresolved problem could be tackled next day. It puts things in a different perspective and often gives one a chance to say, 'Look, I'm sorry I blew up at you, but this is what was happening,' or, 'Let's talk this thing out in a cooler frame of mind'.

Writing a life story is one way of getting things straight in your mind and in the minds of others, and *it does not always have to be published*. Have you ever thought that, as you get older, you become the all-important link with the past for younger generations. Only the present older generation can tell young people what it was like when a farthing was legal tender, when trams were still part of many towns' transport systems. Or what it was like to buy groceries in a small shop

with a solid wooden counter holding rows of large biscuit tins
ranged along the front and sacks of sugar at the back.

Memories are Important

Such memories will be precious to your descendants. It can
be very frustrating to go, as I have gone, from one elderly
relative to another asking for information about marriages,
places of birth, types of work, and other information that is
both interesting and important to younger members of a
family. My own background is fairly mixed incorporating
Angelsey Welsh, North West Yeoman stock, a smattering of
French from the Languedoc area, German Jew, and Spanish
Gypsy, all well mixed with a smidgen of Irish and a bit of
Scots. Trying to untangle that lot is something that is still
exercising my spare time, such as it is. If only my parents or
some of my elderly aunts had kept diaries, or some form of
written record it would have been much easier. Few people
keep diaries these days, and no one keeps letters at all,
indeed, few people write them, preferring to talk on the
telephone, or even via computer and modem.

The act of writing your life story is one way, and a very good
way of setting records straight for your family. For
remembering old friends and faces perhaps long forgotten
and events that were important and changed your life from
that moment. By setting them down you can see your life at
a glance: when you have said or done things you have since
regretted; or when you were made very happy by another
person's help or support. You will begin to see a pattern
emerging and an overall trend of events that has shaped and
forged your personality up to the present time.

Anyone can write their life story without being a literary
genius. To be honest, few published biographies are works of
genius, even fewer make good reading, and those that do are
full of natural sparkle and a sense of that person having lived
to the full and enjoyed both the good times and the bad.

All you need to do is to write as if you were telling your
grandchildren what it was like when you were young.
Imagine their faces and just begin. Never mind about spelling
and grammar – you are not aiming for a Pulitzer, but for a
living record of events that will be passed on to those who

come after you. You can start at any time in your life, and keeping adding to it as the years pass. Spend a few days roughing out an overall plan and breaking down your life into early childhood, school days, teenage years, young adulthood, marriage if applicable, birth of children, early struggles to survive the hazards of family feuds and rows with the in-laws. Deaths and partings, illnesses and holidays. This is the stuff of memory. This is why such a banal programme as *This is your Life* is still running after heaven knows how many years, because people love to know about other people's lives. Your family is no exception, and long after you have gone they will be able to read your words and go over the events, hopes, joys, fears and laughter of your life as you lived it. Besides helping you to prepare for your passing, you will leave something infinitely precious behind for those you love, your own words and thoughts about the life you lived.

Such a record will also help you to put many things into perspective. It may help you to right a wrong, speak words of forgiveness, seek out someone you have not thought about for years, but who was once dear to your heart. It will revive memories and ease old hurts, pour balm on still raw wounds and recall the long hot summer days of youth. When you arrive at the point in your life when feel you have reached the end of your record, try typing it if you can, or get someone to do it for you. It will cost very little to get the typed pages bound together with a soft cover in a ring binding. Now you can read it over quietly and laugh and cry over it. Believe me, you will be fascinated by the life of this person who has lived your life, you will hardly recognize yourself in those pages. When you have read it, put it aside and give thanks for those events, they are the experiences that have moulded you. Then give it away to someone who will take care of it and pass it on. You no longer need it.

Give it Away While You Are Still Here!

Your next task, when you have reached this stage, is to make a will, unless this has already been done, and then you can begin to enjoy yourself. There will come a time when the things you have collected and cherished through your life begin to loosen their hold on you. Look around you and see how much you have accumulated over the years and assess how much it still means to you. Draw up a list of what you think you can bear to give away right now; the chances are you will keep adding to it. Think for a minute: you are into your golden years, your memories are far and away the most precious things you have so you do not need to have so much physical clutter around you. Make a second list of your favourite people and spend a happy few days deciding who will have what. It may be that you will decide to just give away some small things: pieces of jewellery; books; pictures; small ornaments; things that have a story behind them. If you like, write out that story even if it is only a few words, telling the recipient how you came to have this object, if it was a birthday gift, who gave it to you and when, and so on. Ask people round to tea and give them their little gifts, explain that you would rather have the joy of giving things to them now when you can see their reaction and share their delight than leave it until you have gone.

If you wish to give something to someone but cannot bear to part with it just yet, tell them it is theirs and give them a letter to that effect, or write it into your will, but ask them to leave it with you for a while longer. You will find that having made up your mind to give it, the object will soon cease to feel as if it is yours and you will be able to pass it on happily. Always ask the person if they would like to have what you have chosen for them, and make sure they know they can say truthfully if they really want to have it. This ensures that something you have treasured for maybe fifty years does not get sent to the local church jumble sale the moment you have gone. If there are things no one really wants, but which you wish could have a good home, put a small advert in your local paper, or a postcard in a shop window offering to give it to someone who will treasure it as you have done.

If all else fails, give it to the jumble yourself, or to a 'Bygones' shop. Believe me, something so loved will always find a home, and it may be that if you set it free in this way it will come back to you in another life. All treasured antiques have been owned by people who valued and loved them at some time or another in the past. Bless them and let them go and, if you like, stick a small label on the bottom giving a bit of the article's history for the new owner to read and wonder at. Gradually wean yourself away from possessions and reduce your dependence upon them. It will make it a lot easier when it is time to go on. Everyone has certain things that they find hardest of all to give away; for me it will be my books. My library has been built up for over forty years at the time of writing and grows at the rate of some one hundred books a year. Some are old and quite rare, some are purely and simply dear companions, like my treasured copy of *The Ship that Flew*; a battered leather-bound Shakespeare that went through drama school with me and was a gift from someone who had it since he was a boy; first editions of Joan Grant's books given to me as a teenager and now worn thin with much reading. These are things I will find it hard to part with, and yet I know they must go. In my travels I have collected and been given many things, some of which are already earmarked for certain people, while others will soon pass into new hands and I will have the pleasure of seeing them used and loved. Their inner and higher images will still be with me, for even inanimate objects have a higher form.

Wiping the Slate Clean

If you are allowed the time to do so it is important that you make your peace with anyone with whom you have quarrelled or who has in turn held a grudge against you. If you are elderly, do not leave it until it is too late – call them, write to them, ask them to come to you or go to them. It no longer matters who was right or who was wrong, what does matter is that you clear your hearts and minds with each other.

One of the saddest things you will ever hear are the messages sometimes read out on the radio asking for news of someone long lost to friends and family. 'Will James W . . ., last heard of in 1951 living in Sheffield, please make contact with his sister as his mother is gravely ill', 'Sarah B . . ., last known address Islington, London, may have emigrated to Canada since then, please contact Leeds Central Hospital as soon as possible where her father is dangerously ill.' Such messages carry a wealth of human tragedy that we, the listening public, can only guess at and pray that it never happens to us.

Take the time to sit down and think if there is anyone with whom you need to clear the air, and from this time try hard never to let the sun go down on an angry silence. This is especially so between parents and children, and between siblings. It is all too easy in this modern age of fast transport and violent inner cities to lose someone with whom you have quarrelled and you will never have the chance to make it up. There is an old saying, 'Never let the sun go down on your anger.' It is a good one to remember.

Try never to allow contact with your family to break: it can be all too easy to forget to write or phone especially when there are just a few family members left. Unless you are living close to each other there is a very real danger of losing touch, and maybe ending up as a sad little message on the radio trying to find someone who used to be important in your life.

Make your Goodbyes Now

If you know your time is getting short make an effort to call to you those people to whom you wish to say goodbye. They may have to come a long way, but if it is possible, they should come and if not, a phone call will make a lot of difference allowing much to be said and healed in this way. Try to think of it as a party held for friends before you emigrate to a far country. People often use the phrase 'We will never see her/him again.' That is wrong, as you can never be separated once the ties of love have been made. It is true that you have made similar bonds in the past, and will make others in the future, but that does not mean those you love now will be forgotten and separated from you. You will be closer than you are at present in many respects.

Another way to make your goodbyes to those friends and relatives who are too far away to visit you is by either video or cassette tape. It would be very simple and relatively inexpensive to have a video made in which you can say your goodbyes and express your hopes and wishes for the future of those you leave behind. This means that they will always have a reminder of you to show to your descendants. I so often wish that such things had been available when W.E. Butler was alive so that those who have benefited so much from his books and teachings could have seen the man as he was.

Make use of all the technology that is available to leave behind you a record that will last. You only have to think how marvellous it would be for great-great-grandchildren to see you and hear you speak to understand how much it will mean to them.

4

A Beginning or an End?

I am the Slayer whom none escape;
I am death trod under a fair girl's feet;
I govern the tides of the sentient sea
That ebbs and flows to eternity.
Sir Alfred Comyn Lyall, 1835–1911

The Creator and Humanity

The acceptance of reincarnation is almost total among those working and teaching within the Mysteries, be they called to High Magic or Old Magic. They see around them the evidence in nature and in their own inner visions and experiences within their particular tradition. For them death is an essential part of the Universal Law of Constant Change. The immortality so often averred in occult texts refers to that enduring part of a human being, the primal spark in which is held the all important particle of the One, the Primal Energy Pattern humanity refers to as God/dess. For the Nature Religions the Great Mother is paramount, and as the Giver of both Life and Death it is a valid symbolic figure. But if we look beyond *all* symbols we can find something totally unknowable; something beyond our capacity to understand while encased in the physical world.

Among the many different teachings of occult schools is one that expounds what we might call The Holographic Principle. This holds that the number of particles comprising a physical body is maintained on the higher levels of existence. Thus one's astral body has the same number of particles as one's physical body, but they are finer. Those of the mental are finer yet, whilst those of the spirit are refined still further. Beyond a certain point this continuing refinement of matter moves beyond our ability to comprehend. The body, when no longer inhabited by the spirit, decomposes but the subtle body moves on and eventually arrives at a stage in its evolution where complete and utter Self Knowledge is achieved. At this point each and every particle of that 'body' becomes a holograph of the greater whole.

The One, the Ultimate Being, has no shape or form, It has no sexual attributes, for It is beyond sex as we would understand it, yet It contains within Itself all forms of sexuality. Since we were made in Its image The One must also be composed of billions upon billions of particles, each one of which is The Whole One, making it a cosmic-sized energy pattern of unimaginable power and intelligence. That Intelligence stems from vast aeons of creative experience and self-knowledge. Its abilities, Its powers, are beyond comprehension; we may see and understand It only through reflection: *that which is above is reflected in that which is below.* As Initiates of the Mysteries (and I include the Nature Religions in this category) evolve through many lifetimes, they

Figure 4.1 The Lord of Heaven, Navaho.

prepare their bodies for the Great Change. This occurs when they leave the Wheel of Incarnation and no longer need to use a physical vehicle. At this level they make a full realization of their potential Divinity, knowing without any doubt that they are a part of The One, though as yet they may not be able to utilize this knowledge fully. As Exempt Adepts they now have a choice of going on into the Greater Light, or remaining behind to teach those still in incarnation. Most choose to remain for a while at least. At this stage of their evolution they become the Beings we know as the Master Teachers of the human race. Each particle of their being has become enhanced and is now a complete whole within their Wholeness. In this way the Master is able to teach, guide, be close to and in some rare cases, indwell, those men and women willing to work under their guidance. These contacts may run into many thousands, with thousands more being 'mind touched' on a more tenuous level. The Teacher who once walked the earth is now a Lord of Humanity and has in fact become a reflection of The One on the higher levels. This reflection they mediate down to the levels below.

The Saviours

The Saviours of each Age would appear then to be those who have gone into the Greater Light, become one with The One for a moment in eternity and joined with it. This is actually taught in the Bible when the Nazarene tells those who gather about Him that 'The Father and I are One'. Later, after the Sacrifice has been made, He tells them '. . . touch me not, for I am not yet come to the Father', meaning that he has not yet returned to the One and immersed Himself within It. This is true of all the Saviours who have endured going down into the dark to lift up the life forms of this planet, from Innana and Persephone to Osiris and Yeheshua. Having known the ultimate *at-one-ness* they are forever changed and truly become Children of the Creator, the Sons and Daughters of God. Of their own free will they may once again take on physical form in order to bring about a major shift within Humanity's thinking. Their complete union with the One and the knowledge of their Divinity causes them to become a magnet for those willing to be changed. The intensity of their

Wholeness of Spirit would cause a burn out at a fairly young age were it not for the fact that they are destined to die a sacrificial death. Yet there is one more test that each of them must face, and that is the complete loss of contact with The One. For one moment at the point of Death they must stand bereft of all knowledge of that Divinity within. As The One has been alone since the beginning, so must they face this, their last death, totally alone. This utter desolation of spirit is the last barrier to Godhood, the test of their ability to rely only upon their own strength. It is in this emptiness that we hear the cry, 'My God, Why has thou forsaken me?'

Those of us who still struggle to understand hold on desperately, looking for the promise symbolized by the Tarot Card of the Hermit, that the light will shine for us one day. It may be held by The Three-Wayed Goddess, or The Jackal-Headed Anubis, The smiling Orpheus, or the gentle Nazarene, but it will be there. This is the meaning of the injunction to 'Know Thyself', to know and fully understand that we hold our own Divine Immortality within ourselves. It is this that makes a mockery of physical death. It is the secret that the ancient Initiates were given as they lay sealed within their voluntary tombs waiting for the third day and their own new birth into the light. Death, as an Initiate of the Mysteries sees it, is only an Initiation into a higher knowledge of the Self.

The Mechanics of Death

The actual process of dying, unless it extremely quick and/or violent, may seem to an onlooker to be a simple one. For both the physical body trying to hang on to its life force, and the spirit trying to exit to the higher levels, it often becomes a tug of war. Those who have been trained for this moment can avoid the problem by following a pre-set course of exercises. The higher Initiates withdraw step by step focussing on each one. For those untrained it can be made easier by trying to understand the pattern of death.

Let us take the process stage by stage as one who is either completely untrained or partially trained in the Mysteries may experience the onset of death. The first thing that becomes apparent is the tugging sensation as the spirit begins to free itself. You may feel as if you are being rocked backwards and forwards. There will be small snapping, tearing sounds as the ties between the physical and the subtle bodies give way one by one. There is often a disorientation in the consciousness so that what you are feeling and hearing may seem to be happening to someone else. The whole event may take several hours or even days, but at this moment time is the last thing to worry about; you will soon be totally outside of time. Once you have realized the situation (and unless one is trained to observe this may not happen for some time) and have accepted it, then you can observe each stage as it happens and work with it instead of fighting it.

Among other things you will notice is the sensation of extreme coldness in the feet and lower limbs. This is a natural effect of the body's central heat core closing down. The sensation of coldness will gradually creep up the body and the best thing to do is to relax into it and turn the mind towards the observation of the senses. Each one in turn will begin to close down, the sense of touch usually being the first to go. The dying often ask someone to hold their hand or to embrace them. This should be done firmly and with gentle strength so they can feel the pressure as long as possible and know they are being touched, but one should be prepared for the sense of being touched or held to disappear quickly. Taste and smell are intimately related and usually fail at the same time, but the ability to smell may last a little longer. It is because of this that memories are said to flash before the eyes of the dying, as the sense of smell and the seat of memory are intimately linked together. The scent of flowers, more especially if a favourite bloom is in season, is a great comfort to the one passing over, and the life force of the flowers can often help the spirit on its way. They should, however, be taken away as soon as the body has ceased to breathe, for that same life force can sometimes give rise to a manifestation that would not be in the deceased's best interests at this time.

Sight is the next sense to fail and a dying person will often ask if their friends and relatives are still there, seeking a last sight of a loved face. When dealing with the dying, stand directly in front of them at the foot of the bed, or near enough for them to focus to the last of their sight. Hearing is the last to go and it is of great importance that those with them keep talking long after it seems that they have made the transition.

If you have ever been placed under a general anesthetic you will remember the loud buzzing noise that accompanies your return to consciousness: for the dying this noise is often the last point of contact with the world of the living. Make sure your voice is fairly loud and clear, let them hear their given name being spoken and reassure them of your continuing love for them. Remember they will still be close to their body and their family for some time yet so you will be able to speak to them as if they were still in the physical for some days. Often it is possible, if one sits in quiet contemplation of them and the life you have shared, to find their feelings, emotions, and even words being impressed upon your conscious mind. If so it is very important that you do not allow your natural grief to bind them to this level. Assure them of your love and give them leave to depart to their rest.

Remind them that they have passed through the Gate and that you are allowing them go on into the Light. If they have prepared their 'death working', now is a good time to repeat it aloud as if you are walking the path with them up to the point of departure. When you feel you have arrived at the gate/door/entrance leading on to the next level, leave them with loving words and return to your own level.

It may be helpful to go over the death working a few times in the next couple of days, altering it slightly so that you go to the point of parting and 'see' the departed form coming towards you from the opposite direction and standing a few feet away. Speak to them, reassure them and send them your love and your blessing. Do not, however, do this too often, or after the third day when the body would normally be either buried or cremated. By then the spirit will be close to entering its rest period and should be left undisturbed for several weeks. Often the dead themselves will let you know when they are 'awake' again. From then on you may feel them around you quite often, then suddenly they are no longer there: this means they have fully adjusted and may already have moved on to the next stage of their journey.

What May We Expect?

What of the dead person, what can be expected after the death experience has been gone through? With someone who is not 'aware', their last sensation may have been a sound like cloth being torn, a spinning sensation and a moment of blackness, then the astral sight clears and they can see, if they have not already seen, those who have come to meet them. One may die alone physically, but never spiritually, as there will always be someone there to ease the stress of passing over. This is so no matter who or even what it is, as nothing that has life gives up that life in isolation. A murderer paying a price for his crime, his victims(s), an elderly person with no family, a stranger or an amnesiac in a hospital bed, an animal dying on a vivisection table, or in a trap, a soldier on a battlefield – it makes no difference, they will not die alone.

We will go into the passing of an Initiate later on, but for now let us concentrate on those who, although they may be more aware than some are not as yet able to pass over in full consciousness. Here the death working can be of paramount importance and it will help the deceased to orientate themselves at their new level of existence. I have already given full instructions in my book *Highways of the Mind*,[1] but it can bear repeating. A death working is similar in almost every respect to an ordinary pathworking or guided meditation, with one important difference. You do not come back. Everyone has a place where they have been happy or where they would like to have lived when alive: a house, or dwelling of some kind they have always wanted, perhaps in a particular location. When newly dead the first thing needed is a place *to be*. The death working provides that and also a distinct pathway to it, with an equally distinct point of departure.

As an example, one might have always had a dream of a cottage overlooking a lake with a garden that slopes down to the water. From the cottage door is a paved path leading to a gate from which, in turn, a narrow road leads one through a tree-lined avenue towards a broad main road. This road will symbolize the physical level. Between your inner level location and this road there is a high hedge over which you cannot see, but set into it is a door on the physical side of which there is either your name, or a personal symbol that you can recognize.

While still in the physical body, and this can be set up years ahead of when you might reasonably expect to use it, you can pass freely back and forth between this level and the inner one. You can prepare and extend your cottage and its surroundings, making them just as you wish them to be. While you are still alive the door in the hedge will remain open all the time, allowing you to pass in and out. After your death, however, it will be closed, symbolically meaning that the way back to life for that incarnation is closed.

This is a simple example and one may build two or three such locations, chopping and changing until you find just the right one to please you. The whole thing is built and programmed to begin working as soon as death becomes imminent. If you pass over too quickly to work it, then this is where you will find yourself and where you can recuperate for a while before going on. If you have time, it can be worked many times in the days preceding death right up until the moment when the door swings shut behind you and you understand that you can no longer return to the physical level.

You will still be able to reach your family until your body is disposed of, after which time it will be time to return to your prepared place and rest. What may happen then? Usually your cottage or whatever will become a point of focus for those you have loved and who themselves have already passed over. You will see them and talk to them and in general go through a period of rest and recovery. But there will come a time when you will feel restless and want to leave your little haven and this means a new level of awareness is beginning to open for you. From then on you will find yourself going further and further afield until one 'day' you will not return to that location, you will move on, and it will dissolve back into Astral Matter. By then you will be strong enough to face what Dion Fortune called 'the Second Death'.

The Death of an Initiate in the Western Mystery Tradition

Such an Initiate will have prepared the death working long before and worked out exactly how they wish the remains to be disposed of and where. If death comes quickly whether it be a natural or a violent death they will know enough to recognize its imminence: whether it is best to fight for life, or if this is the time to flow with the experience and spring free of the physical body. At the risk of scaring those who dislike flying let me use this example: if you are at 40,000 feet and your plane breaks up, fighting to keep your body is going to be a pretty futile objective. Let it go and head for your Rest Location.

Most likely you will be sufficiently experienced to exteriorize and take a good look at the physical and decide if it is going to be worth fighting for. If not, then you can begin the withdrawal process. The symptoms will be exactly the same as those I have already described, but you will be able to help yourself far more and observe, even with some interest, each stage as it happens. This is even more possible if the death process is drawn out and you have time to go through the whole procedure.

Some years ago in Holland, a young woman dying of leukemia expressed a wish that her journey towards death be filmed day by day so that others could observe the end as it crept closer and learn not to be afraid of its implications. Over a period of months this incredible young woman allowed herself to be filmed as she grew steadily weaker. Her family joined with her in the making of the film and their courage and strength added to the impact of the film. Her final moments are truly beautiful and gentle and the film is an impressive document of the death process. If you wish to have a copy of this film there is an address at the end of the chapter to which you may apply for a copy. The Foundation that produced it, the Humanistische Omroep Stichting, has kindly allowed the name and address to be included in this book, and will gladly answer requests.[2] I must warn you that the dialogue is in Dutch, but the images will tell you all you need to understand. The S.O.L. is hoping to have the sound track translated by one of our Dutch students but this will take a little time.

We will suppose that you, as an Initiate and hopefully full of years and wisdom, are entering your final days. You may be in hospital or in your own room at home, or indeed you may be able to get about almost to the last few days. Your doctor, if he/she is a true friend, will have told you how much time you may expect. Select someone not of your family, but who is preferably one of your own Lodge or School to act as a counsellor. Their work will be to visit you as often as you wish, to be a phone call away day or night, and to give you, always, the truth. Record, or have them record your death working if this has not already been done.

Clear the last of your small possessions, those you have not already given away. Keep a tape recorder near you and each evening, or whenever you feel you would like to say something to someone, tape it. Always begin in the morning by recording the time, day, and date and go on from there. (this is a good idea even if you are not facing the final exit, to keep an ongoing record of things you would like to say to your family and friends and build up a set of tapes they can play again and again when you are no longer with them).

Write to, call, visit if you can make it, those friends you would like to see for the last time. If you cannot go to them, they may be able to come to you. Ask your Lodge Brethren to visit you and maybe hold a short ritual or at least take a last pathworking together. It might be nice to throw a small party to celebrate your 'emigration' to a New World. The church is always telling us what a wonderful place Heaven is, so why does everyone mourn and moan about going there? Make sure you have no debts – not in money, although it is nice to clear those as well if possible, but in kind. Clear away old enmities, hurt emotions and ruffled feelings long held within. You need to go with as little in the way of emotional luggage as possible.

Make sure that each day you have some time to be by yourself in order to think things over and to prepare yourself for the final days. Write or record your thoughts. Go over your life moving backwards to your birth, for you are going towards a different kind of birth into a different kind of existence. If you wish to have the consolation of your church ask the priest to call, or if you have another tradition ask a priest/ess or one who holds a similar position to come and talk to you. Do not try to wrest 24 hours out of each day, forget time, eat when you want, rest when you want, talk and enjoy yourself as you want, in short live normally but with a deeper intensity. Look and listen, touch, taste and smell, use all your senses to the full during these last days.

The Royal Road

There will come a time when you can no longer move around and are confined to bed, so your counsellor should now come more often. They will act as the Psychopompos when the time comes. If it is possible they may like to have another person to help them. Keep your room fresh and sweet-smelling with herbs and flowers. It is not a good idea to use a strong incense at this time, but if you must use it, then choose something light. You will find that sleep comes and goes lightly. Do not force it, you really do not need much of that kind of rest now. Keep to the discipline of having time to yourself when you can think and prepare. Practise opening the power points of the body: 1. the Feet; 2. the Genitals; 3. the Solar Plexus; 4. the Heart Centre; 5. the Throat Centre; 6. the Third Eye; 7. the Crown of the Head. These centres or chakras will be the Royal Road out of the body. Open and close them several times a day, just for a few minutes. Imagine them filled with light, beginning with a light of your favourite colour in its deepest shade, and each time you open make that shade lighter and lighter until it is pure white.

Holding the Memory

Your intuition will tell you when it is time to begin the final phase. Ask to be bathed from top to toe including, unless it is too painful or tiring, your hair, with salted water. Both the salt and the water should have been blessed. The bed and your clothing should be fresh and clean. Feel with all your senses just how your body is reacting: are you warm, hot, or cool? Ask for something light to eat or drink and hold the memory of the taste, listen to the voices around you, or to a favourite piece of music, something you really enjoy. If you can manage it chant the old Calls softly or ask for others to do it. Hold the hand of someone you love dearly, and in between times hold something smooth and pretty to look at, a crystal, or a piece of smooth porcelain or alabaster, and hold the feel of it in your memory. If it is warm enough ask for the window to be opened so you can smell the air and the earth. If this is not possible ask for something like lavender on a handkerchief and lock the scent away in your memory. Look at the faces around and record them, hold them, be determined that you will be with these souls again in some future life. Link yourself to them with bonds of love. Be alert to all that happens, do not allow yourself to drift into unconsciousness if you can help it.

The Call

Now is the time to call for the inner level helpers, who will already be waiting close to you. Begin to look for them, seek to become aware of them. At first you will see them only fleetingly, just as you turn your head, as someone moves aside, in a doorway or by a window. Later you will see them clearly, waiting and smiling and getting ready to help you through the Doorway. Call for those you love who have already passed, or perhaps the Inner Plane Master of your Temple or Lodge. There may be a teacher you once knew at the beginning of your mystery training, or a member of the Lodge now passed. Call and call strongly and they will come.

NOW DO I, . . . (mystery name), CALL TO THE LORDS OF LIGHT TO AID ME IN MY PASSING. GATHER ABOUT ME O YE JUSTIFIED ONES AND BEAR ME FROM THIS PLACE THAT I MAY GO FORTH IN JOY AND HOPE. SO MOTE IT BE FOR THE FIRST TIME OF ASKING. COMFORT THOSE I LEAVE BEHIND ME THAT THEIR GRIEF MAY NOT CALL ME BACK. COME YE GREAT ONES, COME YE LORDS OF FLAME, FORM, MIND AND HUMANITY, BY MY RIGHT AS AN INITIATE I SUMMON THEE TO MY SIDE. SO MOTE IT BE FOR THE SECOND TIME OF ASKING. LET THERE BE RAPHAEL BEFORE ME, AND GABRIEL BEHIND ME, MICHAEL UPON MY RIGHT SIDE AND URIEL UPON MY LEFT SIDE. SO MOTE IT BE FOR THE THIRD TIME OF ASKING. LET THE GREAT PENTACLES OF POWER SURROUND ME AND THE SEVEN-RAYED STAR SHINE ABOVE ME. SET ME FREE SOFTLY AND GENTLY. SO MOTE IT BE THIS LAST TIME OF ASKING. I GIVE THANKS FOR THIS LIFE AND THE LIVES OF THOSE DEAR TO ME. IT IS DONE. ETA MISSA EST. I DEPART IN PEACE, LOVE, AND UNDERSTANDING.

Bring to mind the Doorway or Gate of your death working and place its image at the back of your mind. Now concentrate on your physical body for the last time as it enters its last phase of this incarnation.

The Ending

As soon as you begin to feel the coldness in your feet, open that centre and concentrate on it, realize that your higher self

is beginning to ease out of the shell. If those around you are
also of the Mysteries then a low-voiced chant on one note is
helpful in keeping open the centres. As each centre is opened
and the chill advances the note should go higher until with
the octave the soul is released. As the coldness leaves the feet
on its upward journey say goodbye to the earth that these feet
will not touch again. Open the Genital Centre as the cold
approaches – your counsellor will help you by touching you
and asking if you can feel the touch and by telling you what
is going on around you. Try to focus on each centre as it is
opened and passed over. Realize that you are now leaving the
creative part of your physical self behind, and get ready to
open the Solar Centre. When this part is reached you will feel
the cold at its most intense for this is where the core of body
heat has its furnace. By now you will have begun to feel and
to hear a snapping sound as the ties that hold the physical to
the subtle body begin to tear loose. You may feel as if you are
being rocked gently backwards and forwards. Allow the
sensation to impinge on your awareness but keep your mind
focussed on what is happening. Keep looking towards those
who are here to help you, they are the inner plane midwives
for this kind of birth.

Open the Heart Centre and allow the cold into it. You have
now reached halfway in freeing yourself from the physical,
and will feel the cold less now. You are moving closer to the
head and leaving the more physical lower body. Listen to the
chanting, keep your mind fixed on the changes working
through you. Open the Throat Centre. You will be beyond
speech now and will no longer need it. There may be a loud
tearing sound as the last ties give way, the light will fluctuate,
the sound will change to a loud buzz. Try to keep focussed
and open the Third Eye Centre. At this point you will be able
to see with the utmost clarity those who have come to be with
you at your birth into the Light.

The light will now begin to grow very bright and you will
no longer be able to see physically, but the sound of the voices
and the chant will still be clear. You may hear your given name
being called for the last time, open the last Centre and at the
same time hold to the memory image of the Gate you built
for your death working. You will feel yourself spinning and
then a loud popping noise and you will know now that you
are free. The Silver Cord may wreathe around you, you will

see it growing thinner in one place and finally breaking or being cut by one of the gathered priesthood. Now you are truly free. Ahead you will see your Gate. Go towards it, you will sense on either side those who have come to welcome you. When you reach the Gate go through. *DO NOT LOOK BACK, DO NOT TURN BACK, GO STRAIGHT AHEAD TOWARDS YOUR PLACE OF REST.* You have said your goodbyes while you were still in the body, you do not need to say them again, or to return even briefly to that level. You have no need to attend your own funeral, you have attended them in your lifetime, you know what this one will be like – after all, you arranged it. It is important at this time that you do not allow yourself to be drawn back by the grief of others. You are free, but you need to rest, so think of it as being on holiday. Sit down and relax. Your friends on this side of life will help you to adjust. Now go back over the life you have lived – not too deeply, but enough to lock in the memories perhaps well enough for them to persist into the next incarnation. Then allow your first sleep on this side to claim you. You have earned it.

Rest assured that those you have left behind have their work to do but, and this you must understand, what they do will be more for their benefit than yours. You are already here, alive and well, or rather, dead and well. They need to mourn and show their feelings through ceremonial and grief; it no longer concerns you. Later, when they and you have had time to adjust you can return to reassure yourself that they are all right. Believe me, it is harder for them than for you.

1 *Highways of the Mind* by Dolores Ashcroft-Nowicki. Published by Aquarian Press, 1987.
2 *Humanistische Omroep Stichting* Postbus 135–1200 AC Hilversum, The Netherlands.

PART 2

THE LORE OF PERSEPHONE

5

Honouring the Dead

From the Silence of Time, Time's Silence borrow.
In the heart of today is the Word of Tomorrow.
The Builders of Joy are the Children of Sorrow.
William Sharp, 1856–1902

Preparation of the Body of an Initiate

Method One

In the days before Funeral Parlours and Chapels of Rest, the local midwife, the district nurse or the family themselves did the laying out of the dead. Once the doctor has confirmed that death has taken place the body can be released to the family. Unless there is a local law against it, there is no reason why the family should not prepare the body themselves should they so wish. However, it is not a pleasant task and few would be willing to undertake it, unless it is the body of a beloved child, especially one of tender years whose mother may wish to perform this last task for her child supported and aided by her family.

If you wish to prepare the body yourself then you might wish to ask the district nurse to assist you in the basic details. Body fluids must be prevented from leaking which means all the body orifices have to be well and solidly plugged. It must be washed, including the hair if necessary. Since hair and nails continue to grow after death a man may need to be shaved, and the nails of both sexes clipped short.

For the body of a woman, especially if the coffin is to be viewed by friends and relatives prior to burial or cremation, a light make up may be applied. Whatever is done, see to it that all is done with taste and with love and respect for the physical shell of the departed.

A large new white sheet can be placed in the coffin in such a way that the body may be wrapped in it completely once it is dressed and anointed. Then the procedure may begin with calling on the Lords of Light to be present to witness the preparation of the Initiate for the last journey and to add their blessing of the discarded physical shell to your own.

Please note that only Initiates should be allowed to prepare the body of another Initiate by either of these methods.

Now it is time for the family or those called upon to attend their Lodge companion in death, to perform the sealing of the body with anointing oil and its dressing. In the case of an Initiate this would mean first, a plain white cotton under-robe, and then the Lodge robe over it with the cord of their grade, a Lamen fashioned from felt or wood on their breast, then plain white socks or knee length hose, and sandals or slippers on the feet. If the robe has a hood then it should be drawn up over the head, if not then a simple circlet made from suitable material and inscribed with the mystery name if it is known, or at least the initials. If neither are known to the family then a symbol such as the Alpha et Omega, the Hebrew Letter Shin, a Pentacle, or an interlaced Triangle will suffice. If part of the dead person's regalia included a cloak, this may also be used, though such a piece of equipment is usually passed to a brother or sister of the Lodge.

Instructions may have been left to include the Wand and other items of ritual use within the coffin. These wishes must be carried out no matter how much it may be regretted by others. The Initiate will have had a good reason for these instructions.

A series of symbols inscribed on vellum or parchment should now be placed over each of the sacred centres as follows. Below the feet, or alternatively inside each slipper, a small flower to symbolize the earth they have left. Over the genital area a coiled Ouroboros or snake, tail in mouth. Over the Solar Plexus place either a sun symbol or the Aesculapian symbol of the snake coiled about a staff, then over the heart an Ankh or an Eye of Horus. Cover the throat centre with a star, the circlet will be enough for the third eye centre, and at the very top of the head, where the fontanelle is found in a new born child, a small piece of linen soaked in anointing oil and marked with the Hebrew Tetragrammaton.

The soles of the feet and palms of the hands may also be anointed with oil, then sweet herbs sprinkled over the body. Lavender, hyssop, thyme, rosemary, and rue are good choices, and may be used as lavishly as possible. Mix in with the herbs a good handful of incense grains, as fine a quality as you can afford. Finally a small silver coin may be placed in the hand or under the tongue, and perhaps a small picture or statue of a Godform or Master with whom the deceased felt particularly in contact may be placed on the breast. The white cloth may now be folded around the body and sealed with sealing wax and stamped with a sacred mark of some kind, or if the deceased had a personal seal or one of the School or Order this may be used. This method will suffice for both an interment or a cremation.

Method Two

Seven Initiates are required for this method. Begin by invoking the four Archangels of the Quarters and the Four Kings of the Elements, by name. The latter are needed because the 'contract' between the dead and the elements which held the body together is now void and they need to reclaim them.

If the body has been washed and prepared by the undertakers, known as morticians in the US, the Rite of Preparation may begin. Those performing these last tasks for the deceased should wear white cotton robes that can be burnt afterwards, as well as plastic aprons and, of course, surgical gloves. Their heads should also be covered. While they are working, selected prayers or psalms of the Tradition should be repeated (see last section Prayers for the Dead).

Now the openings of the body must be sealed magically. These differ according to the tradition or even the Lodge/Temple/Order. Usually it will be as follows. The Fontanelle, the Eyes, the Ears, the Nostrils, Mouth, Anus, Penis or Vagina/Urethra. Others may include the navel and may use a strip of parchment that takes in the whole genital/anal area. If the tradition is Qabalistic or Hermetic, then an appropriate seal inscribed upon parchment should be used. If Wiccan, pagan or other magical tradition then there are other symbols that are appropriate and may be used (see last section). A flour paste may be used to hold the seals in place.

All seals should be drawn on vellum, parchment or on squares of new cotton with ink and not ball point or felt tip. Those for the ears and nose may however be impressed on to small disks or plugs of wax and inserted with tweezers.

The Head seal
The Tetragrammaton formed in this way.

For the Eyes
The Hebrew Latin AYIN (eye).

For the Ears
The Hebrew letter DALETH (door).

For the Nostrils
The Hebrew letter ALEPH (ox = breath).

For the Mouth
The Hebrew letter PEH (mouth).

The Genital strip should cover from the Anus to the Navel. This should be inscribed onto a strip of cotton, and care should be taken that the seals cover the area for which they are intended.

Once the seals are in place those present form a circle around the body and place hands on it. Now they chant softly the words *Agla, Aglatah, Aglahim*. This will summon the archangels whose work is to protect the soul of the Deceased. Now those present must be placed at special points, one at the head, one to each hand, each foot and one in the area of the navel. All should have a phial of anointing oil which is now rubbed gently and reverently into the body. As they perform this task they should chant the sacred words of their Tradition, be it Christian, Pagan, Egyptian, Templar, Celtic, Wiccan or any other. Suitable words for this part of the ceremony can be found in the last section. The remaining person should stand aside and intone prayers and invocations to the ancient ones, the angelics, and Godforms known to the dead person. Suitable oil would be Ambergris, Sandalwood, Cedarwood, Oil of Tiphereth, Juniper, Lavender and Sage mixed.

When this has been done the six should stand back while the seventh Initiate makes the sign of the Tradition (Pentacle, Equal Armed Cross, Circled Cross, Ankh, Star, etc.) over the body with a wand or athame. Then the body is turned and the anointing with the oils is continued as before, after which the seventh Initiate again makes the sacred sign over the body, and it is turned back.

Chanting of the invocations should now begin again, and the body can be dressed with white socks, the white cotton inner robe and the deceased's Lodge robe on top, slippers are last. The arms are crossed in Egyptian fashion over the breast or, if preferred, simply arranged to hold the wand, athame, or statue of a godform. Sprinkle rose water, herbs, and a mixture of blessed water and salt around the coffin before placing the body inside. The six now stand in a circle around the coffin holding lighted white candles, while the seventh circles the body censing it with incense, offering a prayer of thanks for the life of the dead person and blessing its spirit. Bless also each of the Archangels and Elemental Kings by name and dismiss them with the traditional: GO NOW TO THINE OWN PLACE. PEACE BE BETWEEN US AND THEE. BE THOU BLESSED TO THE AMOUNT THOU ART ABLE TO RECEIVE. SELAH, SELAH, SELAH. Finally, all seven say: THOU GREAT CREATOR, THOU HAS MADE THE SPIRIT OF THIS MAN/WOMAN, TO BE AS A SPIRIT OF FLAME

AND FORM AND MIND. LET ALL BE DONE ACCORDING
TO THE LAW.

Interment or Cremation

It is up to the deceased or the family to decide how to dispose
of the body. Interment is traditional and many families have
a specific plot or sometimes a vault in which the dead are
placed. Cremation is the most hygienic and it has the added
value of not taking up ground that can be better used.
However interment means that the body returns its nutrients
to the earth. For some religions cremation is required, for
others it is expressly forbidden. For the smaller religious
groups such as the Parsee, disposal can be difficult since their
faith requires that the body is placed where it can disintegrate
naturally in the open air. In their native lands the dead are
placed in a Tower of Silence. To the best of my knowledge,
there are at the moment no facilities for this kind of disposal.

Even among those who work within the mysteries there can
be a morbid fear of being buried alive. If this is a worry then
a clause in the will can instruct the family doctor to make quite
certain there will be no waking by the simple expedient of
opening a vein, piercing the heart, or by other means. Though
it may seem strange, a lawyer will tell you that this often forms
a part of instructions when a will is made.

Cemeteries, as places specifically for burial, have not been
in use for very long, and are in fact fairly new, dating from
the early 1800s. Before that time the only place one might be
buried was in the local church yard. In early times, in out of
the way places, the dead were often buried under a tree, or
in a ditch, in fact anywhere that looked out of the way and
convenient. When large numbers of people died at one time,
for example on a battlefield, of plague or some natural
disaster, a large pit filled with quicklime was usually their last
resting place.

On large country estates where a private chapel was often
built onto the house, a family vault was the preferred method
of burial, and this is still practised today among many of the
titled families of England. Our Cathedrals hold many tombs
of the past Kings and Queens of England and the great men
and women who served them. Some of them are works of art

in their own right, beautifully carved in marble and alabaster. There are several quite famous cemeteries in and around London where famous people are buried. The best known are Highgate Cemetery, Bunhill Fields, and Kensal Green. All three hold the tombs of the famous, the infamous and the ordinary. Death comes to us all no matter how famous or how lowly we may be during our lives. At the moment of birth and at the hour of our departure we are all the same, bringing nothing with us, and taking nothing when we go.

Time to Mourn

Mourning is purely for those left behind, the dead having passed beyond the grief the mourners feel. All that the wearing of black accomplishes is to show the world, and the neighbours, that you have lost someone to the Reaper. In actual fact, if you believe wholeheartedly in what both the orthodox and the esoteric priesthoods tell you, you have not lost them, you have only lost sight of them for a short time and you will be close to them again. True mourning, the need to express one's sorrow over the loss of someone held dear is both natural and healing. Those who rigidly hold their grief in check will find that the tension created will come out in other and less healing ways, whilst those who mourn only to show the world a painted face of grief will not be mourned at all when their time comes.

People will always deal with death in their own ways, by silence and solitude, by crying bouts, by an inability to sleep or, conversely, by sleeping more than usual. The latter can be a signal to consult a doctor as it may be an early sign of depression. No matter how one looks at it, the grief is for one's *own* loss. The departed have gone through the Gates and are resting, they are now in a situation where they are fully aware of the inner reality. They will not be mourning but rejoicing in their new-found freedom, whether it be from pain, a badly damaged body, or an old and infirm one. To wish them back to face those things is not only selfish, it is indefensible.

Where the death seems to have no reason or even a cause, such as infant cot death, or the sudden and accidental death of one dearly loved, the need to mourn and the experience of mourning may have a deeply traumatic effect upon those left behind. In either case there is often a reluctance on the part of friends, neighbours and acquaintances to talk about the newly dead. 'I don't know what to say', is the remark most often heard. The fact is that you need to listen more than you need to speak. Most bereaved families need to talk about those they have lost, to look back over the time they have had with them, to reminisce, sometimes over and over again. Let them, listen and add your own anecdotes to theirs, remember the dead in their place in your life and share it with the immediate family. If it is your own family then share with each other your thoughts and memories of those passed into the Light, but do not bottle it up inside you. The memory of the times you have had with those passed over is a precious gift not to be underestimated. Bring to mind each and every time you have had with them and let the mourners know that you remember with love. Don't tell them that 'time will heal'; we all know it will but we also know that the memory and the sense of loss will never fade. 'You will forget in time', is another favourite saying, but it is not possible to forget someone you have loved deeply, so do not try.

The Death Feast and Other Customs

In many primitive societies Death is celebrated and grief expressed by the giving of a Death Feast. Although such practices are fast dying out, there are still regions where it exists today. The Feast can be as simple as an offering of plain rice wrapped in a leaf and placed on the grave or shrine of the dead, or it can become a celebration lasting for many days and feeding all and any who care to come. It can put severe financial pressure on the family and even put them into debt for many years.

The custom of providing food for both the living and the dead is almost as old as the rite of burial itself, and one aspect of the Death Feast most common to all is that of inviting the Dead to their own Feast. Sometimes two or even three such banquets are held at very specific intervals. In general it takes about one year and several feasts to pacify and send the spirit onwards. In New Guinea the first feast, called a 'bowa' is held the second day after burial, then another on the fourth day called a 'venedari'. The third feast takes place six months later and is called an 'ita'. It is only after this third feast that the widow may come out of mourning.

Sometimes a wooden image of the dead is put up at the head of the feasting and food is thrown to it with the words, 'This is for you, I feed you although you are dead so do not harm me'. This practice and others similar are found in the histories of the Melanesian peoples all over the Pacific. In a few areas the feasts are held every fifth day after burial up to a hundred days. The living are so frightened of the power of the dead that they will go to great lengths to bind them to their own spirit world. This might include the sewing up of the mouth, the dismembering of the body and its burial in pieces over a wide area. Even, in more ancient days, the cooking and eating of the body by the relatives was seen as one way of rendering it harmless. Thus the Dead Man became the actual Feast, providing, as it were, the main course. The guests believed that they were taking into themselves all the good features of the dead such as courage, bravery, and strength.

The Sin Eater

Surviving in Ireland, the North West of Scotland and in some parts of northern England until the latter part of the nineteenth century, and into the late thirties in the most isolated country areas of Ireland, was the tradition of the Sin Eater. Here the traditional Death Feast was given a new and slightly macabre twist and meaning. There were many variations in its preparation and performance from place to place but the basic format remained the same.

The corpse was laid out in different ways according to the location, sometimes directly on three wooden boards laid across three chairs or stools. At other times it was placed in an open coffin supported on trestles. A plain board covered with a white cloth might be laid over it, or again the cloth covered body might have the 'feast' placed directly upon its cold breast. In some it would merely be a circle of bread pieces placed on the forehead. The face, with a copper coin on each eye, was then covered by a small linen cloth. This last part may be linked to the ancient Greek custom of the obolous or coin for Charon the Ferryman of Dead Souls.

Sometimes tradition demanded that the best fare that the

family could provide was spread upon the corpse cloth. New baked bread, butter, cheese, perhaps a small piece of meat or fish, and something to drink – water or milk was the usual, but just occasionally especially in Ireland there might be a small glass of Poteen. In other areas the fare was much simpler, a plate with new baked bread, some salt, a glass of water or milk, with a few coins under the plate.

The Sin Eater was called to eat and drink the food provided, using the body of the dead as a table. In return for the meal plus the payment of the coins the Sin Eater would take the sins committed by the dead in life into himself via the Death Feast. This, so tradition held, would release the newly dead from all sin and allow it to proceed to Heaven. It may readily be seen that this tradition has some elements of more ancient Death Feasts within it. Moreover it has been combined at some stage with a mixture of other beliefs that have filtered into usage over many centuries. For example, that of the Saviour taking the sins of Mankind upon Himself and transmuting them within the Divine Spirit. There are also traces of the communion and Last Sacrament services to be found here. In fact the more one goes into the tradition of the Sin Eater the more one realizes that we have here what even a theologian would admit is a Christ-like figure.

Consider the facts. There is the corpse laid out, with the bread and salt and water resting on the body. Then we have the Sin Eater, sometimes a mendicant figure or an outcast, an untouchable, one who is set aside by reason of the work or service he performs. This person comes to the house of the dead and eats bread and salt and drinks water and in doing so takes away with him the sins of the dead. This frees the deceased who may then pass directly to heaven, leaving the Sin Eater to bear the weight of the dead man's past misdemeanours. Just as the Christian Saviour descended into Hell to release those imprisoned there, so the Sin Eater releases the soul from sin. We may also trace the 'setting aside or the being made outcast' way back to the Sem or Sacrificial Priest in the temples of ancient Egypt. They were also seen as being set aside from their brethren because of the nature of their calling.

In some areas in Ireland there appear to have been what might be termed professional Sin Eaters, that is, one person who acted as the Sin Eater in a small community. But in other areas it was sometimes a traveller, a stranger passing by who would then take the sins far away. Or it might be someone in need of food and a few pence – a beggar, or a tramp. In rare instances the practice of Sin Eating passed from father to son and the whole family was shunned by the villagers who would cross themselves when meeting them, saying:

> The cross of the nine angels be about me,
> from the top of my head
> to the soles of my feet.

William Sharp, under the pen name of Fiona Macleod, wrote many deeply moving tales of nineteenth-century Highland life. In a story called 'The Sin Eater' he gives a telling description of the scene as a local man, returning the Highlands after years of exile, is prevailed upon in his need of food and money to Eat the Sins of a man he hates. The essentials of the story are as follows:

The corpse was laid out upon three boards placed across three milking stools and covered with a sheet of canvas. The son of the dead man brought a saucer and placed it upon the breast of the dead, and into the saucer he placed a thick piece of new baked bread and some salt. Then another saucer of water. The Sin Eater points out that to be totally effective he must eat it from the actual naked breast of the corpse, whereupon the canvas is rolled back and the dead man's shirt opened to allow the saucers to be placed on his bare breast. In silence and with care salt is sprinkled under and over the bread, and into the water.

The Sin Eater took the saucer of water and held it before his lips saying, 'Away all the evil that is upon thee, and may it be upon me and not upon thee, if with this water it cannot flow away.'

The water was then passed, sunways, three times over the head of the corpse, then he drank from the saucer as much as his mouth could hold, and poured the rest over his left hand, letting it fall on the ground. Then he took the bread and this was also passed over the head of the dead man three times as he said: 'Give me thy sins to take away from thee. Lo, as I now stand here, I break this bread that has lain on thee and I am eating it. In that eating I take upon me the sins of thee, O man that was alive and is now white with the stillness.'

The Sin Eater then broke the bread and ate of it, thus taking upon himself the sins of the dead man. The remainder he crumbled and threw upon the ground and trod it in.

In the story it goes on to tell how he is banned from working in the area and is named as 'The Scapegoat'. Because of this he refuses to pronounce the traditional last words of the Sin Eater which are (to the corpse), 'His share of heaven be his' (to the son) 'May God preserve you,' and (to the others), 'God's Blessings upon this house.' Instead he pronounces a threefold curse: 'Bad Moan be upon you, May you drift to your drowning, Wind without direction to you, God against thee and in thy face, may a death of woe be yours, Evil and sorrow to thee and thine.'

For those with a love of the Highlands and their traditions the works of Fiona Macleod are well worth the effort of searching for them in second hand book lists. You will also find a good example of Sin Eating in *Precious Bane* by Mary Webb. [1]

Funeral Games

Some burial customs require not only a feast, but the keeping of the body, well wrapped in several layers of cloth, leaves, and river mud, for up to a year, usually in the rafters of the family home. Only then is it taken with great ceremony and in procession to be buried in a small cave that is then tightly sealed.

In Rome the Death Rites were not only celebrated at the burial but also during the Dies Parentalia, a nine-day Festival during which the burial rites of one's departed parents were renewed. Offerings of milk, honey, oil and even blood were made to the dead and the tombs decked with flowers, greeting those passed on with the words, 'salve sancte parens'. During these nine days the temples were closed, no one could get married, and the city's magistrates were not allowed to wear their insignia.

Funeral Games were also a way of honouring the dead, especially among the Greeks and Romans, and when a hero died it was long a custom to organize such Games in his name. Wine was offered at the beginning of each race or event and spilled on the ground for the dead to drink. The winner offered the honour given to him to the dead hero as a gift, hoping in this way to partake a little of his courage and bravery.

Most of the ancient societies believed that the most urgent wish of the dead was to return to the land of the living. To prevent this people went to a great deal of trouble. During the May Festivals the male head of a household got rid of any ghosts that might be hanging around by spitting black beans at nine spaced intervals right around the house, then calling out, 'Manes exite paterni'. This could be called an early exorcism! There are records of the Funerary urns being connected to the upper surface by lead pipes. Libations of wine, and a mixture of milk and honey were then poured down on to the actual remains. This caring for the Ancestors by keeping them well supplied with food and wine is a direct link back to the earliest times when the dead were buried with food and weapons for their journey to the Land Beyond, indicating a firm belief in survival after physical death.

Ancient Egyptian Preparation of the Dead

In Egypt the preparations for the well-being, satisfaction, and happiness of the Dead were the most elaborate of all. As a race they believed absolutely in an Afterlife and made elaborate preparations for it. For them everyone was born into the world with a sort of alter ego called a 'kha'. This kha lived with the physical self as long as life lasted. At death it left but, it was believed, returned to the body if that body was preserved. Statues and drawings of a person's 'kha' were placed in the tomb and drawn on its walls so that the consciousness of self, the 'identity' was not lost. (This fear of the loss of identity is still with us thousands of years later.)

At death one embarked upon a long and dangerous journey to the Halls of Judgement where, in the awesome presence of the Forty Two Assessors, the heart of the deceased was weighed and judgement pronounced. If one passed the test then one became an 'Osiris', and went on into Amenti. If not, destruction awaited the soul in the form of The Devourer.

The 'kha' lived in the tomb with the preserved body and because it needed sustenance it became the practice to leave food and wine and beer at intervals in a specified area within the complex of the tomb. In this way contact between the living and the dead was maintained, following traditions that were old before the pyramids were built.

The process of mummifying a body was enclosed within seventy days of ritual following on one from another. From the house where death had occurred the body would be taken to an 'ibu' or tent of purification. Although buildings were used for the process of embalming and preserving the dead, a tent could be easily moved from place to place. This enabled those who were the forerunners of modern day funeral directors to be mobile. It was also much cooler to work in and there was the added advantage that the circulation of air through the tent allowed any unpleasant smells to be blown away.

The priest who overlooked the whole process, the Controller of Mysteries, wore a Jackal mask, emulating Anubis the God of embalmers, cemeteries, and tombs. He was also the guide of the dead accompanying them on the journey to the Halls of Judgement. Another priest would stand by and recite the long prayers and invocations needed to keep away demons and those spirits that gathered around the newly dead.

The body was thoroughly washed with water and natron, and all through the process it would be washed many times, as absolute cleanliness was important. Once washed it would be taken to the place of embalming, called a 'wabet', and here the internal organs were removed. The brain was usually taken out through the nose by means of two different instruments, one hooked, and the other with spiral shaped handle and a small cup at the end.

Once the brain had been completely removed the cavity was washed out and the next part began. The mouth, nose and ears were plugged with either wax or oil-soaked linens, the face coated with a paste made from resin and wax. Each eye was covered with a piece of linen and the eyelid carefully drawn over it. The body would now be turned onto its right side and the Jackal-headed priest carefully drew a line on the left side of the body.

Waiting outside was the priest who would now perform one of the most unpleasant tasks but also the most important one. He was not allowed into the area until called and he was usually a man of some strength. His implement was a stone knife often referred to as an Ethiopian Stone, honed to extreme sharpness. On being summoned he would enter and, using the drawn line as a guide, he would cut deep into the body. Through the cut he would draw out and sever each of the major organs with the exception of the heart. These, the liver, the stomach, the kidneys, intestines and the lungs, he would wrap separately in cloth previously soaked in resin, and place them in four waiting canopic jars. Now, his task done, he would be chased from the room by the other priests with shouts of derision and anger. Like all sacrificial priests he was considered unclean, but he was also essential.

We may pause here and reflect on the fact that this casting out of those who perform the tasks others cannot or will not do is an incredibly ancient tradition. We may link it with the ritual Scapegoat, both animal and human, with the Sin Eater whose acquaintance we have already made. We might say that Cain, the 'slayer' of Abel, was such a one, along with those whose unenviable task it is to betray, slay or cause the death of those destined to be among the great Teachers of Humanity. There is room for a lot of thought here, and the piecing together of bits of ancient knowledge.

The body was now washed again, this time with palm wine, and the incision was ritually closed with a wax plate bearing the symbol of the Eye of Horus. Each toe and fingernail was wired in place and the next phase began. This was the drying out of the body with the use of natron, a naturally occurring salt of sodium carbonate with some sodium bicarbonate, additional sodium sulphate and sodium chloride. There is evidence of other types and mixtures having been used, but natron itself can be found in the delta area around the Wadi Natrun, north of Cairo. The corpse was laid on a sloping bed, several types of which have been found and displayed in museums. The body cavities were filled with the drying mixture and finally the whole body would have been covered with it.

It took around forty days, or six weeks to completely dry out and then the business of wrapping the body would begin. This would take place in the Per Nefer or House of Beauty. Perfumes and oils would be rubbed into the body to make it supple and also to enable the embalmers to pad out the body if this was necessary. The bandaging took many days, as many as twelve or fourteen, because rituals and invocations were being carried out all the time. At little as 200 or as much as 1,000 yards of linen would be used, sometimes painted with prayers or information about the life of the dead person. In between the layers the masked priest would place amulets, jewels and magical papyri.

The head was wrapped first, extending to the neck and shoulders to keep the whole top of the body in place. Fingers, toes, and male genitals would be wrapped separately, followed by the arms, legs, and finally the trunk. Now layer after layer was wrapped around the whole body, the priests pausing now and then to cover the linen with scented reins, gums, and oils. The position of the arms varied, either crossed over the chest or at the sides or, in the case of men, over the genitals. Finally, holding bands of linen would secure the whole thing in place. The 'mummy' was now ready to be placed in its sarcophagus.

Now a different priest took over and the rituals moved to the waiting tomb. Incense was burned, wine and water offered and invocations chanted. Finally, the high point of the whole seventy days of mourning and ritual culminated in the ceremony of 'Opening the mouth'. With a ritual adze the priest opened the eyes, ears, nose and mouth. In fact, he restored to the dead man his ability to use his senses. He was now equipped to begin his journey to the Halls of Judgement where he would answer the questions of the Forty Two Judges of the Dead.

The Practice of the Wake

The Irish Wake is more of a send-off party than a mourning as death is seen as the beginning of a new and wondrously different state of existence. The corpse in an open coffin, laid out in its best clothing, is the centre-piece of the whole celebration. Relations, friends and neighbours, to say nothing of the odd stranger, drink to the passing and the future well-being of the departed. If the celebrants end up as incapable of movement as is the corpse, well then, 'tis a grand way to go.

During the latter part of the last century, the final resting place in rural areas was often a long way from the homestead. As there were few alternatives to human muscle power for carrying the coffin, it was a wearisome business, needing frequent stops along the way to bolster the flagging energy of the bearers. One delightful Irish story tells of a tavern situated at a crossroads playing host to several funeral parties while the coffins and their occupants filed by the door, waited patiently. In a spirit of brotherly love, everyone drank a toast to their own and everybody else's departed, not once but several times. The result of which was none of the coffins got buried in the right graves or mourned by the right families. But, as one character said, what does it really matter, they were all mourned and missed just the same, and the Lord God knew who they were.

The Death Watch

In many traditions it is the custom to watch over the dead until the burial or disposal of the body. In modern times we see this most often when a member of a Royal, ruling, or presidential family 'Lies in State'. It may also be that a member of an old and noble house will be watched over by those who knew and worked for the family for many years. In the case of the former it is usually the members of the services that provide the Death Watch, standing at the four quarters with their arms or swords reversed. In the latter it may be farm workers, game wardens, ghillies if the family is of Scottish blood, or even male members of the household staff.

If it can be arranged, which usually means if the Bishop will allow it, it is a signal honour to be placed, the night before burial, in the church with a guard around the body. However it is a tiring watch and it needs to be changed every hour for the pressure of standing still in one position, as well as the very real psychic pressure of the atmosphere, can be quite overpowering. Those people with a high sensitivity should not undertake a Death Watch unless they have been trained in the control of their psychic abilities. It is often the case that the dead will watch over their physical shells along with the living, saying goodbye to something that has served them well and given them great pleasure.

1 *Precious Bane*, Chapter 4, Mary Webb. Published by Virago, 1978.

6

Wraiths and Shadows

I know no birth, I know no death that chills;
I fear no fate nor fashion, cause nor creed,
I shall outdream the slumber of the hills,
I am the bud, the flower, I the seed:
For I do know that in whate'er I see
I am the part and it the soul of me.
John Spencer Muirhead

Death Omens and Second Sight

More often than one may think, the warning of death is given to certain families and, on occasion, to people who may avoid the arms of Persephone if they take heed of it.

In the Highlands especially, where the veil is thin between the levels of existence, there are many who are forewarned of a passing. It is locally known as *Taish na Tialedh*. Indeed the Celtic race are more than usually endowed with the 'Sight', and nowhere more than in the western reaches of Scotland and Ireland and the northwest areas of England and Wales. Nor is this to be wondered at for the West has always been the Place of the Dead. Amenti, Elysium, The Isles of the Blessed, Tir-nan-Og, Hy Brasil and Avalon, have all at one time or another been seen and spoken of as the place where the dead find their rest.

We may divide true second sight from the more often found presentiment, though it is true they both often overlap. In the former, 'sight' is actual – the pictures, images, visions are seen with the objective eye. A presentiment is more often a feeling of gloom or dread that almost everyone has felt as sometime or another. We are concerned here with only those instances that foretell death, and there are many that are well documented.

R. Woodrow, in his book *Analecta*, tells the story of a Highlander talking with the Provost of Glasgow while standing by the Cross of Edinburgh. When a stranger walked by the Highlander told his companion that the man would soon be dead, and indeed the stranger was within minutes run down by a carriage and killed.[1]

It is again in the misty land of the Western Isles that the phantom funeral may be seen as a foretelling of a death to come. This is unusual in the sense that the full cortège is seen by the psychic, with every person who will attend that funeral in their place, and the coffin open to show the face of the dead.

This gift of the Sight is given mainly, it would seem, to those from the north and the Western Isles of Scotland, but in the Lowlands on occasion the death warning is given. A farmer's wife living in a small village near to Kelso was looking out of her window when she saw a funeral cortège approaching. She called her sister to come and see but when the sister looked there was nothing there. Again the wife looked from her window and saw it (the funeral) coming down the road and again called her sister, but she could see nothing on the road. At the third time the woman said, 'It will be here soon', and threw her apron over her head and began to wail. Half an hour later the farm servants entered bearing her husband's body, for he had been killed an hour before by a fall from a farm cart.[2]

In 1912 a minister of the Scottish Kirk went to visit a young parishioner who was thought by his doctor to have 'the consumption'. On arriving at the house he saw a gathering of men in black surrounding a hearse. He entered the house and asked the mother why she had not let him know of the young man's death. She gave a shriek and exclaimed, 'He is not dead, but you have seen the wraith funeral.' The boy died the following day.

The Death Knocks

Wales has a similar kind of phantom funeral but they also have something called the *Tolaeth*. This is a series of knocks on the door or window and is peculiar to the north of Wales. I can vouch for this myself, as I have heard the *Toleath* many times when a member of my family has died or is about to die. Where the *Taish na Tailedh* impinges upon the sense of sight, the *Tolaeth* affects the psychic ear. One uses the clairvoyant faculties and the other the clairaudient.

There are various kinds of *Tolaeth*. One may hear the sound of furniture being moved around, as if to make space for a coffin, or it may take the form of footsteps coming to the door, which is sometimes knocked upon loudly. Again I can vouch for this, for in the cottage in which I lived as a child, the approach of phantom footsteps up the path and three strong knocks upon the door was something I heard not once but many times as I grew up. But then, on my mother's side most of my ancestry is from the isle of Angelsey in the north of Wales.

Sometimes the *Tolaeth* sounds very near, even on the table while one is eating, and the air in the room goes very cold. At times there is an echo to the sound as if it comes from a large and empty tomb. In 1878 there was a train accident involving much loss of life. A few days before the crash one of the victims was sitting with his wife when they heard the Tolaeth sound on the door, and heard footsteps climbing the stairs. Within 48 hours they brought his body home to his wife. This incident was recorded at the time by a local paper, *The Western News*.

The *Teulu* or Goblin funeral is another portent of a coming death that is peculiar to Wales. It travels down the darkened road with every appearance of being real, until one can see through the figures as it passes. One of the strange things about this form of the sight is that it can be transferred to another person if the Seer places their hand upon your shoulder. Then you would see exactly what they see.

Returning to Scotland we have the Phantom Piper that heralds the death of chieftains of certain clans, and the great Black Dog that appears to sit and howl outside the gate of a certain noble family when its head is about to die. At the moment of death of one of these Lords in Egypt, his dog began to howl way back in England.

The Corpse Candle

The Corpse Candle as a Death Omen is recorded all over the British Isles. It is usually seen emerging from the room in which the death will take place and, floating a little above the ground, marks out the route of the cortège until the place of burial is reached. It is said that the size of the candle is an indication of the age of the victim, and that when it is white it will be a woman that dies, red if it will be a man. In Wales this death light is referred to as *Tan-we* or *Tan-Wedd*, or as the *canwyll y corph*.

The Beansidhe and
The Washer by the Ford

Among the best known death omens are the Banshee (or *Beansidhe*), the Death Fairy, and The Washer by the Ford. The former is usually attached by tradition to a family and when one is about to die she will sit by the door and wail their death. Sometimes she can be seen as a dark misty cloud surrounding a tree or a bush near to the door or gate. At other times she will manifest as a white-shrouded, haglike figure that rushes hither and yon. Occasionally she will sit by the fire and weep quietly.

Although often it is only the family that hear her wails, at times others with the Sight or the Hearing can be drawn into the experience. Once and once only I heard a *Beansidhe*, and I never in my life want to hear that horrendous eerie sound again. I was walking along an ordinary road in the far north of Wales and stopped to take in the view over the sea to where I knew lay Ireland. The day was fine and sunny with a blustery wind, then it began to grow darker. With a startling suddenness the view I was seeing changed and became stiff and painted, like the frame in a film when it is stopped. Even the leaves on the trees stopped tossing in the wind. From across the sea, from the direction of Ireland came a thin high wail that increased in volume and horror until I felt my eardrums would burst. All the pain and sorrow of Hell was in that sound, then it stopped as suddenly as it had come. That was the day Lord Mountbatten and his grandson and others died at the hands of terrorists. There is not tradition of a *Beansidhe* in that family, but that day I heard one. I do not wish to hear another.

The Washer by the Ford is found in both the Western Highlands and Ireland and strikes terror in the heart of those who meet her. She is always found standing by the river bank or in the water washing bloodstained clothes. There are two aspects to the Washer, one as a foreteller of death, and one as an aspect of the Goddess. Both aspects would need a book to themselves to do them justice.

All Hallows Eve

Tradition tells us that on the Eve of All Hallows Day the dead are allowed to return to their homes and their loved ones. It is a time when both worlds meet and for a moment can commune. For those who follow the ancient ways, Samhain is one of the great Sabbats, when the dead are invited to share the feast, to draw near to the fire and to look upon their families once more.

In many countries the Feast of the Dead is a time of festival and rejoicing, when food, drink and candles are taken to the cemetery and the whole family make it a party time. Skulls made of sugar and marzipan are sold and cakes in the form of coffins, skeletons and tombstones are made and eaten.

The party will last until just before dawn when the living and the dead take their leave of each other until the next year. Sometimes they will take a person back with them, one who is perhaps ready to leave the body behind. For some of course it is a night of witches and demons and all things that are evil. But if one is afraid of those who once loved you on the physical level then where is the All Consuming Love of that One who descended into the dark after His own death and brought life and light to all?

For those of us who know the old traditions, their worth and their overflowing love for the earth and all that lives on it, it is a time to reflect on the passing of yet another year. A time to prepare for the Death of the Horned God, whose proud antlered head will go down into the earth to await his awakening by the Spring Goddess. The festival of Samhain is one of promise; a promise that is kept in the renewal of life.

Death is also a festival of promise; a promise that you will return when the time is right and live again. If you have the faith of the caterpillar you will take on the shroud and prepare to build your wings.

The Second Death

When the soul moves out from the physical body its first need is to rest, for death can be as exhausting as birth. There is the trauma of the last few weeks or days before death and the pain of parting from those you love. Now is the time to recuperate and it is for this reason that the Initiate builds the 'death working'. Here, in surroundings built from the astral matter and conforming in every way to the ideal as it was visualized, the newly passed soul may do as it pleases. Nothing is impossible, all is accomplished by the will. But rest is the most important and there is time to reflect over the life you have lived.

It is possible that one may be sent to you to help you remember everything in its correct order. Or perhaps a past brother/sister of your Order or School will come. As you become accustomed to your astral body, which is usually a younger version of the one you had in the immediate past, you are able to withstand the facing of the Records. This is a detailed 'viewing' of your last life, every small happening, every word spoken, every lie told, every wrong deed and right deed displayed. This is where you have to face up to things, to admit where you were wrong and ask forgiveness, make plans to readjust the Scales.

It is not a pleasant task. No matter how good a person you think you were, there will be things you have forgotten or perhaps did not even notice at the time. Things of which you will be ashamed and which will make you cringe. There will also be things that will make you glad and happy. Not just once but over and over again you will sit through the viewing of that life until every last bit of it is understood, experienced and assimilated.

During all this time you will have to be exploring your surroundings as well, learning about the Laws of this level of existence and how to cope with them. Your friends and helpers will be there to assist. It may be that during this time you will be summoned to the passing of someone you love. This will be a joyful meeting and you will be able to help them as others helped you. You will have time together to enjoy the closeness and love you had before. But you will have to understand that there will be a time when you must, for a time, part again. They may have other paths to tread before you meet once more. But you will always be able to reach out to them.

Then one day will come a big realization, you no longer have a recognizable body. In fact you do not have a body at all. The usual thing is to panic and hurriedly make yourself a body in which you hide, trying to convince yourself that you are really there. You were there anyway even without the body, but it did not seem that way at the time. You have now come through the immediate period of adjustment and it is time to go on. Time to face The Second Death.

That sounds scary and perhaps it is at the time, but you must put your trust in those around you. It is at this point that you may realize that the Beings who are around you now are different to those who were around you last time you looked. They are more essences than bodies, you can feel rather than see them. Understand them rather than hear them. Be part of them rather than touch them. Up until now you have had first, a physical body, then, after death, an astral/etheric body. You had the last one because it helped you to adjust to your new surroundings better, but you really do not need a body in this next level. You are on the edge of moving into a new and higher level where you will no longer need any kind of body.

Every part of you will want to hang on to the form you are still wearing at this time, you will want to fight to keep it, and this is perfectly natural. However, you can't keep it. Sooner or later you are going to have to take that next step. It might as well be now. This is a leap of faith and although it will seem, for one split moment that you are alone in that immense void, it will not be so.

Passing Into The Light

Let yourself be drawn into the Light that is before you. It will feel a little like falling into the sun, in fact your thoughts may indeed make it look like the sun. Do not let fear take hold of you, you are following a path you have taken before in other deaths, so try and remember how it was then. Allow the form you have been using to melt away and return to its natural state of astral matter. You will not need it, at least not for a while, unless you have passed the need to incarnate again.

There will be a new lightness of Being, a feeling of freedom that is unutterably sweet. Open your spirit sight, not your eyes, as you no longer have eyes in that sense. Open your sight and look around you. It will take you some time to adjust but the first thing you will see are those Beings who were invisible to your astral sight. They have been with you all the time.

There may be a feeling, a need to stay close to the place where the levels overlap. Try to overcome this and allow your new companions to ease you further into this new phase of life. You will find that all your senses work on this level as easily as on any other, only differently. Your sight is the most immediate: it is more than seeing, it is pure perception. You can see the infrastructure of everything around you. You can 'perceive' it on all levels right down to its primal atom and up to its perfected ideal. You can 'hear' in the sense that everything is vibrating at the rate set for it on this level, so you will not only hear those vibrations, you will be able to see them. Imagine, you will be able to *see things becoming as they move through the levels*.

Taste and scent will intermingle to allow you to combine their essences; touch is a state of mind, you do not touch it, it touches you and becomes part of you. The Beings around you are all vibration and rhythm, they are manifesting anew in each moment, and so are you. You are in a state of continual becoming, you are at the point of Kether.

In this state of being to which you will gradually become accustomed, you will begin your learning process. In the astral state you went over and over your past life learning its lessons. Now you will learn how to apply those lessons and how to formulate the beginnings of a new life that will incorporate the understanding you have gained at this level. You may find yourself waiting by the barrier with others like you, to help other newcomers through that first plunge. If you have gone beyond the need to incarnate again you will be offered a choice of going further into the Light, passing through successive levels of learning and gaining wisdom and understanding until you pass beyond anyone's ability to know or understand what it is you have become.

If, as is most likely, you need to return to earth then there will come a time when the learning and the teaching begin to slow down. You will find yourself at some point in the rhythm close to that area where once you feared to cross over. Maybe you will feel the same fear again, but fear this time of losing the freedom you have at this level. But the pull is too strong and you will inevitably be drawn over the barrier between the world of the mind and the world of the astral. Your immediate feeling will be of intolerable heaviness, of weight and weariness. Again, there will be companions about you to help. Your first task will be to build up the semblance of the new body you will be using. Then gradually, with help, you will piece together the conditions of the new life that will soon be yours. You will know what your main objective is to be in life and to achieve this you will need to select the environment and the parents, the conditions and perhaps the handicaps or struggles you will need to overcome. Gradually the waiting life will become more and more real until you realize that your surroundings have become dimmer, that you are not as free as you were. You are drawn towards a certain place that looks familiar.

The earth is below you, it spins slowly, you see the area in which your new life will begin. You drift nearer, closer, until you can see the great vortex of force that will be your entry into life once more. You will be loath to leave your present condition, but perhaps you will meet old friends and loves in your new life. The vortex is closer and you are drawn into it, you spin endlessly down into warmth and weight and darkness. Perhaps there is a moment of pain or discomfort, then just an enclosing love. You are on your way again.

1 *Second Sight: Its History and Origins* by Lewis Spence. Published by Rider, 1951.
2 *Folklore of the Northern Counties* by W Henderson.

7

The Sacred Duties

Hail O ye who make perfect souls to enter into the house of Osiris;
Make ye the well instructed soul of the Osiris, The Scribe Ani
whose word is true, to enter in and be with you in the house of
Osiris. Let him hear even as ye hear; Let him have sight even as
ye have sight; Let him stand up even as ye stand up; Let him take
his seat even as ye take your seats.

Dirge from *The Book of the Dead*

The Summoning of the Devas

This chapter is concerned with those things that can be done
to help the departing soul on its way, and make things easier
for it. First things first, the cleansing of the room. If the death
occurs in hospital this may prove a little difficult. However, it
is now the practice of most schools offering occult training to
teach students how to work at a purely mental level. If it needs
to be, any and all of the following may be done in this way.
That goes for the following rituals as well. Alternately you
may ask permission of the Ward Sister to draw the curtains
for privacy. You can, quite rightly, say you are performing a
religious rite.

Obviously things will be a lot easier if the event takes place
at home. First, then, the cleansing. You will need salt and
water in two containers, some incense, four candles to place
at the four quarters, plus a small amount of fine earth. In
hospital I suggest you use salt and water already mixed, some
oil of Sandalwood or Frankincense instead of incense and dab
some on the four quarters of the bed itself. Instead of candles
use four small pencil torches, or even at a pinch draw some
candles and colour them. Remember your magical training,

Figure 7.1 Stylised form of Osiris.

'intention is everything in magical ritual'.

Place the earth beneath the sheet and under the person. This symbolizes the Element of Earth beneath. The incense, something light and fragrant to represent the Element of Air above, should be lit. The candles, white, red, green and gold will be the symbol of the Element of Fire. Finally, the salt and water cleansed with the usual prayer [1] and mixed together and placed either side of the head will become the Element of Water.

One person may do this by themselves, or it can be done by four people acting for the Devas and one to do the invoking. Light the candles one by one and invoke the Four Levels of the passing Self.

White: (Light candle) I INVOKE THE HIGHER SELF OF . . . WITH THE LIGHTING OF THIS CANDLE. COME INTO THIS PLACE OF JOY AND PEACE AND BRING WITH YOU THE RADIANCE OF THE SUN BEHIND THE SUN. IN YOUR GLORY COME, IN YOUR BEAUTY COME, IN YOUR PURITY COME. LET YOUR GIFT BE THAT OF LOVE. (If possible the person should answer for themselves, if not let another speak for them.)

Answer: I COME IN GLORY, IN BEAUTY, AND IN PURITY WITH THE GIFT OF LOVE.

Red: (Light candle) I INVOKE THE MENTAL SELF OF . . . WITH THE LIGHTING OF THIS CANDLE. COME INTO THIS PLACE OF NEW CREATION AND BRING WITH YOU THE POWER OF THE WORD. IN YOUR POWER COME, IN YOUR GRACE COME, IN YOUR SWIFTNESS COME, AND LET YOUR GIFT BE THAT OF CREATIVITY.

Answer: I COME IN POWER, IN GRACE, AND IN SWIFTNESS, WITH THE GIFT OF CREATIVITY.

Green: (Light candle) I INVOKE THE ASTRAL SELF OF . . . WITH THE LIGHTING OF THIS CANDLE. COME INTO THIS PLACE OF DREAMS AND HOPE, AND BRING WITH YOU THE WARMTH OF COMPANIONSHIP. IN YOUR GENTLENESS COME, IN YOUR LOYALTY COME, IN YOUR STEADFASTNESS COME. LET YOUR GIFT BE THAT OF BROTHERHOOD.

Answer: I COME IN GENTLENESS, IN LOYALTY, AND IN STEADFASTNESS. WITH THE GIFT OF BROTHERHOOD.

Gold: (Light candle) I INVOKE THE EARTHLY SELF OF . . . WITH THE LIGHTING OF THIS CANDLE. COME INTO THIS PLACE OF DEPARTURE AND BRING WITH YOU YOUR FAITH AND TRUST. IN THAT TRUST BE WITH US, IN THAT HOPE BE WITH US, IN THAT FAITH BE WITH US. LET YOUR GIFT BE THAT OF SERENITY.

Answer: I COME IN TRUST, IN HOPE, AND IN FAITH WITH THE GIFT OF SERENITY.

To the East: I INVOKE THE DEVAS OF THE EAST, TO COME UPON THE WINGS OF AIR. GATHER ABOUT US O YE GREAT ONES AND GENTLY TAKE THE BREATH FROM THE NOSTRILS OF THE STAR BORN.

East Deva: WE COME AS INSTRUCTED AND INVOKED TO BE WITH THE STAR BORN AT THE ENDING. THE BREATH OF THE NOSTRILS WAS OUR GIFT AT BIRTH.

NOW IS THAT GIFT RETURNED TO US.

To the South: I INVOKE THE DEVAS OF THE SOUTH, TO COME TO US UPON THE WINGS OF FLAME. GATHER ABOUT US O YE GREAT ONES AND GENTLY TAKE THE WARMTH FROM THE BODY OF THE STAR BORN.

South Deva: WE COME AS INSTRUCTED AND INVOKED TO BE WITH THE STAR BORN AT THE ENDING. THE FIRE OF THE BODY WAS OUR GIFT AT BIRTH. NOW IS THAT GIFT RETURNED TO US.

To the West: I INVOKE THE DEVAS OF THE WEST, TO COME TO US UPON THE WINGS OF WATER. GATHER ABOUT US O YE GREAT ONES AND GENTLY TAKE THE MOISTURE FROM THE BODY OF THE STAR BORN.

West Deva: WE COME AS INSTRUCTED AND INVOKED TO BE WITH THE STAR BORN AT THE ENDING. THE MOISTURE OF THE BODY WAS OUR GIFT AT BIRTH. NOW IS THAT GIFT RETURNED TO US.

To the North: I INVOKE THE DEVAS OF THE NORTH, TO COME TO US ON THE WINGS OF EARTH. GATHER ABOUT US O YE GREAT ONES AND GENTLY TAKE THE SALTS OF THE EARTH FROM THE BODY OF THE STAR BORN.

North Deva: WE COME AS INSTRUCTED AND INVOKED TO BE WITH THE STAR BORN AT THE ENDING. THE SALTS OF THE EARTH WERE OUR GIFT AT BIRTH. NOW IS THAT GIFT RETURNED TO US.

To All: NOW DO WE PRAISE AND THANK THEE FOR THE BIRTH GIFTS GIVEN WITH LOVE. THEY HAVE BEEN USED IN HAPPINESS AND JOY AND IN HAPPINESS AND JOY SHALL THEY BE RETURNED. AIR TO AIR, FIRE TO FIRE, WATER TO WATER, AND EARTH TO EARTH. SO MOTE IT BE THIS DAY.

All: SO MOTE IT BE INDEED AND FROM THIS DAY.

(Candles are extinguished, the bowls of water removed and poured away and the incense taken away. The earth may remain, and if it can be collected after death, then it should be sprinkled in the coffin.)

The Summoning of the Four Archangels

This may be added to the Devic and the Elemental summoning if it is wished to make a full ritual. They can be

Figure 7.2

spaced by calling in the Archangels first, then opening the quarters and calling in the Elemental Kings, and then summoning the Devas to stand about the bed. The same four helpers may speak for all those summoned and the main speaker stands for the Guardian of the Rite. Then you may proceed with the rest of the ritual.

Guardian: (Makes opening sign) BRETHREN ASSIST ME TO FORM THE PORTAL OF THE EAST. BEFORE US ARE THE GOLDEN DOORS OF THE SUN THAT LEAD TO THE LIGHT. THREE TIMES THE HEIGHT OF A MAN AND SET WITH TOPAZ AND WITH AGATE. SIX IS THE NUMBER OF THE SUN BEING THE SPHERE OF TIPHERETH AND SIX KNELLS ARE REQUIRED TO OPEN THE DOORS OF THE EAST. (Knocks in three sets of two) BRETHREN THE DOORS ARE OPEN AND WE MAY SUMMON RAPHAEL THE ARCHANGEL OF THE SUN.

GOLDEN WINGED ONE, THOU OF THE HONEY SCENTED BREATH, BEHOLDER OF THE COUNTENANCE, HEALER OF THE SICK AND WEARY, THEE WE INVOKE RAPHAEL, SUPPORTER OF THE THRONE. WE SUMMON THEE TO THE SIDE OF THE STAR BORN. . . . TO BE AT HIS/HER DEPARTING. GRANT US THY GENTLE PRESENCE AND BE WITH US IN THIS MOMENT OF JOY FOR THE SPIRIT THAT IS RETURNING TO ITS NATURAL HOME. TAKE THY PLACE AT THE HEAD OF THE STAR BORN AND THERE REMAIN.

All: HAIL RAPHAEL, CHILD OF LIGHT, LORD OF FLAME, TAKE THY PLACE AMONG US AND LEND US THY STRENGTH IN THIS HOUR.

Guardian: (Makes opening sign) BRETHREN ASSIST ME TO OPEN THE PORTAL OF THE SOUTH. BEFORE US ARE THE BRONZE DOORS OF THE PRIMAL FIRE THAT LEAD TO THE PLACE OF CLEANSING. THREE TIMES THE HEIGHT OF A MAN AND SET WITH RUBY AND CARNELIAN. FIVE IS THE NUMBER OF FIRE BEING THE SPHERE OF GEBURAH, AND FIVE KNELLS ARE REQUIRED TO OPEN THE DOORS OF THE SOUTH. (Knocks three times, then twice) BRETHREN THE DOORS ARE OPEN AND WE MAY SUMMON MICHAEL THE WARRIOR ANGEL.

WIELDER OF THE SWORD OF JUSTICE, THOU OF THE

FOURFOLD WINGS OF FIRE, SHIELD OF THE
COUNTENANCE, PROTECTOR OF THE WEAK THEE WE
INVOKE, MICHAEL, SUPPORTER OF THE THRONE. WE
SUMMON THEE TO THE SIDE OF THE STAR BORN . . . TO
BE AT HIS/HER DEPARTING. GRANT US THY STRONG
PRESENCE AND BE WITH US IN THIS MOMENT OF JOY
FOR THE SPIRIT THAT IS RETURNING TO ITS NATURAL
HOME. TAKE THY PLACE UPON THE LEFT SIDE OF THE
STAR BORN AND THERE REMAIN.

All: HAIL MICHAEL, CHILD OF LIGHT, LORD OF
FLAME, TAKE THY PLACE AMONG US AND LEND US
THY STRENGTH IN THIS HOUR.

Guardian: (Makes opening sign) BRETHREN ASSIST ME
TO OPEN THE PORTAL OF THE WEST. BEFORE US ARE
THE SILVER DOORS OF THE MOON THAT LEAD TO THE
PLACE OF RECEIVING. THREE TIMES THE HEIGHT OF A
MAN AND SET WITH OPAL AND MOONSTONE. NINE IS
THE NUMBER OF THE MOON BEING THE SPHERE OF
YESOD, AND NINE KNELLS ARE REQUIRED TO OPEN
THE DOORS OF THE WEST. (Makes three sets of three
knocks.) BRETHREN THE DOORS ARE OPEN AND WE
MAY SUMMON GABRIEL ANGEL OF THE WORD.

MESSENGER BETWEEN THE WORLDS, BRINGER OF
JOY AND HOPE, THOU STAR BRIGHT ONE, PROTECTOR
OF THE COUNTENANCE, THEE WE INVOKE GABRIEL,
MAINTAINER OF THE THRONE. WE SUMMON THEE TO
THE SIDE OF THE STAR BORN . . . TO BE AT HIS/HER
DEPARTING. GRANT US THY GENTLE PRESENCE AND
BE WITH US AT THIS MOMENT OF JOY FOR THE SPIRIT
THAT IS RETURNING TO ITS NATURAL HOME. TAKE THY
PLACE AT THE FEET OF THE STAR BORN AND THERE
REMAIN.

All: HAIL TO THEE GABRIEL, CHILD OF LIGHT, LORD
OF FLAME, TAKE THY PLACE AMONG US AND LEND US
THY STRENGTH IN THIS HOUR.

Guardian: (Makes opening sign) BRETHREN ASSIST ME
TO OPEN THE PORTAL OF THE NORTH. BEFORE US ARE
THE MARBLE DOORS OF THE EARTH THAT LEAD TO
THE PLACE OF RENEWAL. THREE TIMES THE HEIGHT OF
A MAN AND SET WITH ALL GEMS OF THE EARTH. TEN
IS THE NUMBER OF THE EARTH, BEING THE SPHERE Of
MALKUTH, AND TEN KNELLS ARE REQUIRED TO OPEN

THE DOORS OF THE NORTH. (Makes two sets of five knocks.) BRETHREN THE DOORS ARE OPEN AND WE MAY SUMMON URIEL THE ARCHANGEL OF THE EARTH.

GIVER OF BREAD, GUARDIAN OF THE YOUNGER BRETHREN, MASTER OF THE HIDDEN SILENCES OF THE HEART. PILLAR OF ENDURANCE. SWEET SINGER BEFORE THE COUNTENANCE. WE SUMMON THEE TO THE SIDE OF THE STAR BORN . . . TO BE AT HIS/HER DEPARTING. GRANT US THY SUSTAINING PRESENCE AND BE WITH US AT THIS MOMENT OF JOY FOR THE SPIRIT THAT IS RETURNING TO ITS NATURAL HOME. TAKE THY PLACE UPON THE RIGHT HAND OF THE STAR BORN AND THERE REMAIN.

All: HAIL TO THEE URIEL, CHILD OF LIGHT, LORD OF FLAME, TAKE THY PLACE AMONG US AND LEND US THY ENDURANCE IN THIS HOUR.

Guardian: ALL IS NOW READY FOR THE RITE OF DEPARTURE.

The Calling of the Elemental Kings

The Devas are called because they are there at every birth and so need to be at each death. The Archangels are called to open the Doors of the Quarters and sustain both the living and the dying through the last moments of the passing. The Elemental Kings are summoned to help the quick disintegration of the physical body and to return it to its four components.

Each has special work to do and all will be of value. However, if time is short or the full process is too much for the departing, only the summoning of the Archangels need be applied (although as they need do nothing more than close their eyes and rest it is not too demanding on them).

The Elemental Kings are: of Air, Paralda; of Fire, Djinn; of Water, Nixsa; of Earth, Ghob. Their forms are those of Sylphs, Salamanders, Undines, and Gnomes, and they may be visualized in these forms, though human sized. However, they do have other forms and whatever way you wish to picture them, that is the form they will assume. Remember that though formed of their natural element each one of them is an individualized spirit of great power and intelligence. Do not confuse them with those they rule who, although powerful, can only understand what is put to them in terms of their own element. This makes it dangerous to attempt contact with them unless through the mediation of either their King or the Archangel of that element.

If you are preparing a Rite of Departure based on, say, the Egyptian or some other tradition, then you will need to adjust the format of the summoning using the Godforms most suitable to the element. You might select Ra or Osiris instead of Raphael, Sekhmet or Horus for Michael, Isis or Thoth for Gabriel and Anubis or Nephthys for Uriel.

Summoning the Elemental Kings

Stand the representatives of the Four Kings at the head, foot, and either side of the bed, which should be drawn out from the wall to give free access all around. If the weather is warm open the window to let in the element of air. Sprinkle soft, finely sieved earth between two large piece of white paper and place beneath the mattress. The representative of Air should have a bowl of incense, that of Earth should have a small amount of flower petals and grain or rice, the Fire representative should have a candle of rose red in a holder and Water a bowl of salt and water.

East and West should have a white ribbon stretched between them, and North and South a ribbon of red. The Guardian of the Rite should have a sharp knife and a Wand. The Guardian circles from southeast to southeast working sunwards, then southwest to southwest. Then northwest to northwest, and finally northeast to northeast.

Guardian: (Touch the head of the dying with the wand and summon the first King.) KING OF THE ELEMENT OF AIR I CALL YOU BY YOUR NAME PARALDA. BY THIS NAME I BID THEE COME INTO THIS PLACE AND STAND AT THE HEAD OF THE STAR BORN. I CHARGE YOU IN THE NAME OF RAPHAEL THE REGENT OF YOUR ELEMENT THAT YOU HEED MY WORDS AND, IF IT BE NOT AGAINST THE WILL OF THE ONE, TO DO MY BIDDING AT THIS TIME. THAT BIDDING SHALL BE THUS:

THAT AT THE MOMENT OF DEATH YOU SHALL TAKE BACK THAT PORTION OF YOUR OWN ELEMENT FROM

THE BODY OF THE STAR BORN AND SET IT FREE AND
THAT YOU SHALL STAND BY AT THAT MOMENT TO GIVE
COMFORT AND STRENGTH TO THE DEPARTING. SHALL
IT BE SO BROTHER OF AIR?

Paralda: IN THE NAME OF RAPHAEL THE REGENT OF
AIR I HEED YOUR WORDS, AND IN THE BIDDING OF
THEM I SHALL BE DILIGENT. THAT PORTION OF THE
ELEMENT OF AIR I SHALL TAKE BACK FOR MY OWN
AND SET IT FREE UPON THE WINDS OF HEAVEN. I
SHALL OFFER COMFORT AND STRENGTH AT THE
DEPARTING. IT SHALL BE SO BROTHER IN BODY.

Guardian: (Touch breast with wand) KING OF THE
ELEMENT OF FIRE, CHILD OF THE PRIMAL SUN. I CALL
YOU BY YOUR NAME, DJINN. BY THIS NAME I BID THEE
COME INTO THIS PLACE AND STAND UPON THE LEFT
HAND OF THE STAR BORN. I CHARGE YOU IN THE
NAME OF MICHAEL THE REGENT OF YOUR ELEMENT
THAT YOU HEED MY WORDS AND, IF IT BE NOT
AGAINST THE WILL OF THE ONE, TO DO MY BIDDING
AT THIS TIME. THAT BIDDING SHALL BE THUS:

THAT AT THE MOMENT OF DEATH YOU SHALL TAKE
BACK THAT PORTION OF YOUR OWN ELEMENT FROM
THE BODY OF THE STAR BORN AND SET IT FREE, AND
THAT YOU SHALL STAND BY AT THAT MOMENT TO GIVE
COMFORT AND STRENGTH TO THE DEPARTING. SHALL
IT BE SO BROTHER OF FIRE?

Djinn: IN THE NAME OF MICHAEL THE REGENT OF
FIRE I HEED YOUR WORDS, AND IN THE BIDDING OF
THEM SHALL I BE DILIGENT. THAT PORTION OF THE
ELEMENT OF FIRE I SHALL TAKE BACK FOR MY OWN
AND SET IT FREE WITHIN THE CORE OF THE SUN. I
SHALL OFFER COMFORT AND STRENGTH AT THE
DEPARTING. IT SHALL BE SO BROTHER IN BODY.

Guardian: (Touch genitals with wand) KING OF THE
ELEMENT OF WATER, CHILD OF THE PRIMAL SEA. I
CALL YOU BY YOUR NAME, NIXSA. BY THIS NAME I BID
THEE COME INTO THIS PLACE AND STAND AT THE FEET
OF THE STAR BORN. I CHARGE YOU IN THE NAME OF
GABRIEL THE REGENT OF YOUR ELEMENT THAT YOU
HEED MY WORDS AND, IF IT BE NOT AGAINST THE WILL
OF THE ONE, TO DO MY BIDDING AT THIS TIME. THAT
BIDDING SHALL BE THUS:

THAT AT THE MOMENT OF DEATH YOU SHALL TAKE
BACK THAT PORTION OF YOUR OWN ELEMENT FROM
THE BODY OF THE STAR BORN AND SET IT FREE AND
THAT YOU SHALL STAND BY AT THAT MOMENT TO GIVE
COMFORT AND STRENGTH TO THE DEPARTING. SHALL
IT BE SO BROTHER OF WATER?

Nixsa: IN THE NAME OF GABRIEL THE REGENT OF
WATER I HEED YOUR WORDS, AND IN THE BIDDING OF
THEM SHALL I BE DILIGENT. THAT PORTION OF THE
ELEMENT OF WATER I SHALL TAKE BACK FOR MY OWN
AND SET IT FREE WITHIN THE PRIMAL OCEAN. I SHALL
OFFER COMFORT AND STRENGTH AT THE DEPARTING.
IT SHALL BE SO BROTHER IN BODY.

Guardian: (Touches feet with wand) KING OF THE
ELEMENT OF EARTH, CHILD OF THE CREATOR, I CALL
YOU BY YOUR NAME GHOB. BY THIS NAME I BID THEE
COME INTO THIS PLACE AND STAND AT THE RIGHT
HAND OF THE STAR BORN. I CHARGE YOU IN THE
NAME OF URIEL THE REGENT OF YOUR ELEMENT THAT
YOU HEED MY WORDS AND, IF IT BE NOT AGAINST THE
WILL OF THE ONE TO DO MY BIDDING AT THIS TIME.
THAT BIDDING SHALL BE THUS:

THAT AT THE MOMENT OF DEATH YOU SHALL TAKE
BACK THAT PORTION OF YOUR OWN ELEMENT FROM
THE BODY OF THE STAR BORN AND SET IT FREE, AND
THAT YOU SHALL STAND BY AT THAT MOMENT TO GIVE
COMFORT AND STRENGTH TO THE DEPARTING. SHALL
IT BE SO BROTHER OF EARTH?

Ghob: IN THE NAME OF URIEL THE REGENT OF EARTH
I HEED YOUR WORDS AND IN THE BIDDING OF THEM
SHALL I BE DILIGENT. THAT PORTION OF THE ELEMENT
OF EARTH I SHALL TAKE BACK FOR MY OWN AND SET
IT FREE WITHIN THE BODY OF THE EARTH MOTHER. I
SHALL OFFER COMFORT AND STRENGTH AT THE
DEPARTING. IT SHALL BE SO BROTHER IN BODY.

Guardian: (Takes Incense from Paralda and circles the bed
once, then censes the dying Initiate with three swings of the
censer to the head and again to the body. Then sets aside the
censer. He takes the lighted candle from Djinn and circles the
bed once, then passes the candle down and across the body,
and sets the candle down. The salt and water from Nixsa he
sprinkles around the bed once and then over the dying in the

form of an equal armed cross. Lastly with the flowers and grain from Ghob he makes the last circle and sprinkles the rest over the body.) NOW I BID YOU KINGS OF THE ELEMENTS, PARALDA, DJINN, NIXSA AND GHOB, TO DEPART INTO YOUR OWN PLACE WITH THE BLESSING OF US ALL RESTING UPON YOU. PEACE BE BETWEEN US FOR ALL TIME. (He takes the knife and cuts the white ribbon) AIR AND WATER ARE FREE. (He cuts the red ribbon) EARTH AND FIRE ARE FREE. FIAT, FIAT, FIAT.

All Kings: IT IS DONE, BROTHER IN BODY WE DEPART NOW IN PEACE AND JOY.

The Loosing of the Silver Cord

At the moment of death when the spirit emerges from the body the silver cord can be seen quite clearly by the clairvoyant sight. It is in many ways the equivalent of the umbilical cord at birth and it behaves in a similar fashion. For a short while it remains attached to both the spirit and the body, then it begins to thin in one place and will finally break at that point. Sometimes, and it may happen even to an Initiate, the physical body will make a last effort to hold on. When this occurs it may be a good idea to assist the spirit to break off the cord. It should only be done, however, if there is obviously a struggle between the body and the spirit, one to go free and the other to hold on.

Do your best to persuade the resisting body to let go. If this does not help then prepare to loosen the cord ritually. One person should take the head of the dying in their hands, two others stand either side and gently stroke the arms to quieten and gentle the physical self. Whoever is elected to act as the seer should stand at the foot of the bed and compose themselves as if for deep meditation. Use any of the techniques for achieving at least a third level where you will not be disturbed. If the body moves suddenly, do not be disturbed, if it does it is merely a reflex action.

Fix your inner sight on the Solar Plexus area of the body. It will have lost most of the surrounding aura and the colours will be dull and fading fast. However you should be able to see the 'cord' either lying in a coiled circle with one end floating freely or stretched quite tightly and flailing to and fro.

Watch to see if there is a point at which it is thinner than the rest, or darker. When you find it, that is the place to concentrate upon.

Call for assistance by summoning one of the Archangels, preferably Michael or the Godform Anubis. Build the figure as strongly as possible and ask for the cord to be cut cleanly. I emphasize that this loosening is not to be attempted unless there is an obvious struggle and help is needed. When you can see that the cord is severed, bless and dismiss the Forms you have summoned. Do not cut the cord yourself. Those you call are the ones who should perform this task, not a living human being.

1 For the prayer see the section on invocation and prayer.

8

The Way of the Jackal

At The Feet of Isis
Her feet are set in darkness – at Her feet
we kneel, for She is mother of us all –
A Mighty Mother, with all love replete;
We, groping midst the shadow's dusky pall,
Ask not to see the upper vision bright,
Enough for us Her feet shine clear – all virgin white.

Anonymous

The Power of the Voice

Those who serve the Great Mysteries know that the power of
the voice is one of the greatest secrets. But the voice, no matter
how well-trained and perfectly projected, needs words to
match. Words well used are miniature examples of that one
unknowable, perfect utterance that brought our cosmos into
being. No matter how well devised a ritual may be, unless its
words flow deep and strong that ritual will not ignite the heart
and soul of those who work it. Prayers and invocations,
hymns of praise, chants and mantras are not merely words,
each one of them is a sword, a pearl, a song or, sometimes,
a damp squib.

An invocation should reach the heart and soul of those who
listen as well as the one who speaks. A prayer must reach
upward and keep flying on the wings of emotion, or it will
not fly at all. Remember the soliloquy of the King in Hamlet,
'My words fly upwards, my thoughts remain below, words
without thoughts never to heaven go.'

Where prayers and invocations for the dead are concerned
the beauty and care with which they are put together is a

measure of the love one feels for the person passed over. There is no greater compliment, as Victorian ladies well knew, than to have someone write a poem especially for you. The following pages offer a selection that will suit most traditions.

There is no reason why you should not interchange the names of Angelics and Godforms, Devas and Nature spirits from those given here. Some I have found in old books and rituals that have been handed on to me by a variety of people. Many are to be found in poetry books[1] which are unfashionable to read nowadays but which will yield rich rewards if delved into. Many of the ancient hymns of the Mysteries are still in print somewhere, and it adds to your work to use words that were written thousands of years ago. To illustrate my point I have added a small piece of poetry to each chapter to fit in with the theme of the book.

The Christian Tradition

In what might be termed the New Age Religions, many who work High Ritual Magic also acknowledge the Christian *Mysteries*. They pay homage to the Christ of this passing Age, as they do to all who have in their turn taken on that momentous task. It is, therefore, right and proper that it has a place here.

Silent Offer
Alpha and Omega both thou art,
A shining Adonai wrapp'd round with stars
Be aware of me O God, my life is yours
And all that comes of it is but a dream of Thee.
Anonymous, 1931

Prayer before Battle
Here in thy hands O lord behold thy servant.
From time to time and age to age bound just to Thee.
Let all my deeds and joys, and dreams be bounded by
Thy sweet care of me.
Here in thy creation O God, behold thy human son.
From life to life and dawn to dawn aware of Thee.
In all my days of life and nights of death
I am but a part of Thee.
Sgt James Farrell 1943, El Alamein

The Recommendation
These hours, and that which hovers o'er my end,
Into thy hands and heart lord I commend.
Take both to thine account that I and mine,
in that hour and in these, may all be thine.
Richard Crashaw, 1613–1649

My Spirit (an extract)
O wondrous Self! O sphere of light,
O sphere of joy most fair
O act, O power infinite,
O subtle and unbounded air,
O living orb of light
Thou which within me art yet me.
Thomas Traherne, 1636–1674

The Order
Hail, sacred Order of Eternal Truth.
That deep within the soul,
In single Majesty does reign
One undivided whole.
Hail, Intuition pure, whose essences
The central core supply,
In conscience, language, science and certitude
Finds Art, Beauty and Harmony.
After E. Caswell, 1814–1878

The Light of Asia (an extract)
Ah blessed One, O High Deliverer . . .
Lover, brother, guide, lamp of the law.
I take my refuge in thy name and thee.
I take my refuge in the law of Good.
I take my refuge in thy Order, OM.
The Dew is on the Lotus, rise great Sun.
And lift my leaf and mix me with the wave,
Om mani padme aum, the Sunrise comes,
and I, the Dewdrop, slip into the shining sea.
Sir E. Arnold, 1832–1904

Invocation to Osiris
Through the sound of the rising waters I call thee Risen One,
I hear the lamentations of the mourners as they weep for me
My ka has fled into the desert and I am alone.
Stone upon stone my tomb arises and in the Wabet is my body
  laid.
The Guardian of the Rite approaches and calls my name
I cannot answer for not yet has my mouth been opened.
Lift me from this desolation into new life.
Thou art the risen one, Osiris, raise me.

Hymn to Osiris

Hail, royal one, coming forth in the body
Hail, hereditary son, chief of the ranks of the gods.
Hail, lord of many existences.
Hail, lord of the duration of life, giver of years.
Thou art living through many eternities.
Thou art worthy of great praise and rejoicing.
Take possession of thy city O beloved of the Gods.
Thou art the mysterious one, he who is unknown to men.
Anonymous

Hymn to Osiris

Sing we Osiris dead,
Lament the fallen head,
The light has left the world, the world is grey,
About the starry skies
The web of Darkness flies,
And Isis weeps Osiris passed away.
Your tears, ye stars, ye fires, ye rivers shed,
Weep children of the Nile, your lord is dead.
H.R. Haggard, 1856–1925

Funeral Chant To the Beloved for the Last Time

With starlit seas below,
We move with all the suns that move,
With all the seas that flow;
For bound or free, Earth, Sky and Sea,
Wheel with one circling will,
And thy heart drifteth on to me,
And only time stands still.
H.R. Haggard 1856–1925

Within the Sanctuary

Softly we tread, our measured footsteps falling
Within the Sanctuary Sevenfold.
Soft on the Dead that liveth are we calling,
Return Osiris from thy kingdom cold.
Return to those that worship thee of old.

Hymn to Mithras

Mithras, god of the Midnight, here where the Great Bull dies,
Look on thy children in darkness. O take our sacrifice.
Many roads hast thou fashioned, all of them lead to the light,
Mithras, thou a soldier, teach us to die aright.
Hymn of the 30th Legion, AD 350

Hymn to Zeus

Lead me O Zeus, and lead my Destiny.
Whither ordained is by your decree.
I'll follow doubting not, or if with will
Recreant I falter, yet I shall follow still.
Anonymous, c.800 BC

Death Chant
Woman

I am ashes, ashes are earth,
Earth is the Goddess.
Therefore I am not dead.
Corpus Inscriptionum Latinarium Vol VI (Berlin)

Man

I am a corpse, a corpse is dust, earth is dust.
Since the earth is a God, I am not dust, I am God.
Anthologia Lyrica Graeca Vol I (Leipzig, 1925)

Passing Hymn

Lady, my time has run and I approach the end,
Faithfully have I served thee and thy Lord.
Open the secret path between the Rowan trees
that I may pass into the Land of Dreams.
Place three white stones across the stream
that I may cross into thy Queendom.
Forget me not Lady, now that my time is here.
Wiccan prayer, M. Mistlethwaite

Dark Lady

In thy garb of Night I bid thee come Wise One.
You are the ending of us all, come now.
Before thee is one of thine own ready to tread the Path
that leads into the Land of Flowers.
Be gentle sweet Goddess, for we have loved her/him
And part unwillingly and only unto Thee.
Let the passing be swift and full of dreams, and if it
    may be,
Comfort us, who cannot follow more.
Wiccan prayer, Anis Lee, 1924–1981

The Blessing of the Dead and License to Depart

The most important thing for the dead is to go on and not to
look back. This may seem hard, but the sooner they break

away from the tears, mourning and grief that surround the family the better. This does not mean they do not love those they leave behind, simply that they, as Initiates, know that once their Presence is removed the family can rebuild its life.

There are some deaths that leave little or no 'residue', it is as if those people have never been, yet the memory of them is strong and beautiful. They have passed quickly and surely, and often you will find this in older country people who have lived close to the earth all their lives. They have an instinct that tells them to go quickly and not to look back.

Not to look back: that is the key, and it is a hard one to turn, for we all long to linger, to comfort and be with those we love for a last few moments of time. But, as Initiates, we should remember that we are *not* being cut off from those we love, that we will see and be with them again. Although it is inevitable that we will be separated by time and space when we incarnate again, if we have loved truly, then those invisible ties will draw us back to them life after life. How often do we meet someone for the first time and know them at once, and love them, recognizing them with the heart as someone we have known before. Those who know how can call to themselves their loved ones from long ago in the form of children[2] and lovers. The fear of loss is something we must get over if we are to deserve the title of 'Initiate'.

The Blessing

Once the spirit has departed and the cord has broken, those who have come to escort the newly dead will be ready to ease them away from their surroundings. They cannot do this easily if there is a lot of grief around the body. First allow each person to say farewell, then ask them to move into another room, preferably some way away, or even into a garden where the atmosphere is lighter.

Take away all flowers and extinguish all candles, uncover the body and address the spirit and its helpers.

. . . (Speak their given name.) I KNOW YOU ARE STILL HERE IN THIS PLACE, BUT IT IS BETTER THAT, FOR A TIME, YOU GO WITH THOSE WHO HAVE COME TO HELP YOU. I SHALL BLESS AND TEMPORARILY SEAL YOUR

BODY, AND ALLOW YOU TO DEPART. IF YOU SO WISH, THEN YOU MAY RETURN AT A LATER TIME TO SEE YOUR OLD SELF AND THOSE YOU LOVE, BUT AS AN INITIATE YOU KNOW WELL THAT IT IS BETTER IF YOU GO NOW. FAREWELLS HAVE BEEN SAID, DEAR FRIEND GO NOW.

With water and salt sprinkle the body from head to foot.

I CLEANSE THEE OF THE IMMEDIATE BONDS OF GRIEF AND FEAR THAT MAY HOLD THEE, AND IN THE NAME OF THE MASTER TEACHER OF YOUR ORDER I BLESS THEE.

With oil make a sacred sign of your choice, on the forehead, breast, palms and feet of the body.

I SEAL THY BODY AGAINST ANY WHO WOULD USE IT FOR ILL PURPOSE AND FROM ANY LEVEL, AND IN THE NAME OF THE MASTER TEACHER OF YOUR ORDER I ANOINT THEE.

The License to Depart

With the body still uncovered take your place at the foot of the bed. It is important that if possible, you are robed. With a Wand, Athame, or Finger touch the *feet*:

. . . (Given name or Mystery Name if known.) I AM . . . (Give mystery name.) I AM HERE TO GIVE YOU PERMISSION TO DEPART FROM THIS PHYSICAL LEVEL AND PASS ON TO THE NEXT TO REST AND PREPARE. YOUR FEET HAVE LEFT THE EARTH AND NO LONGER WALK UPON IT, THEY NO LONGER KNOW THE TOUCH OF RIVER OR OCEAN, THE WINDS OF EARTH WILL NOT CHILL THEM, THE FIRES OF THE HEARTH NO LONGER WARM THEM. DEPART, I GIVE THEE PERMISSION TO DEPART.

(Touch the *navel* as before.)

YOUR BODY HAS BEEN SEPARATED FROM ITS SPIRITUAL UMBILICAL CORD AS ONCE IT WAS SEPARATED FROM THE BIRTH CORD. YOU HAVE BEEN BORN INTO A NEW FORM A NEW EXISTENCE, A NEW LIFE. DO NOT LINGER. DEPART, I GIVE THEE PERMISSION TO DEPART.

(Touch *breast*.)

YOUR HEART NO LONGER BEATS WITHIN YOU, THE

BLOOD NO LONGER RUNS THROUGH YOUR VEINS, LOVE CANNOT CALL YOU BACK, NOR GRIEF DISTURB YOU. TURN YOUR FACE TO THE LIGHT BEFORE YOU AND ENTER INTO IT FULLY. DEPART, I GIVE THEE PERMISSION TO DEPART.

(Touch *head*.)

YOUR SENSES NO LONGER RESPOND TO THE EARTH PLANE, THE BODY YOU INHABITED IS NO LONGER YOUR PLACE OF LIVING. YOUR TIME IS PAST AND A NEW FUTURE AWAITS YOU. YOU HAVE LIVED OUT YOUR TIME UPON EARTH, YOU HAVE BEEN AND STILL ARE MOST DEARLY LOVED. YOUR DEEDS WILL LIVE AFTER YOU. I THANK YOU IN THEIR NAME FOR ALL THAT YOU HAVE GIVEN TO OTHERS. I BLESS YOU FOR WHAT THERE HAS BEEN BETWEEN US. I STAND WITNESS TO YOUR LIFE. I AM GLAD THAT YOU WERE BORN. DEPART, I GIVE THEE PERMISSION TO DEPART. IT IS DONE, IT IS DONE, IT IS DONE.

Cover the body, bow to the four quarters and leave the room. No one should go in for some hours, thus giving the deceased time to fully withdraw.

It has been the private practice of my husband and myself for many years to light a candle whenever someone of note has died. We give thanks for their life and always add the 'permission to depart'.

There are personalities we all know and love whose death takes a little away from us. The sadness felt by millions of people at the deaths of Winston Churchill and George VI, for example, was very real, so too at the passing of figures beloved for their gifts of laughter and skill. Comedians Tommy Cooper and Eric Morecambe will not be names known to many outside the UK, but they meant a lot to us, and we mourned them sincerely. In Olivier we lost a great actor and the rest of the world sorrowed with us, and when finally God calls home his film 'alter ego' George Burns, England as well as America will mourn him. Keep a large candle in a special holder and when disasters strike light it and offer a thanksgiving for the lives they have lived. Let it not be a prayer for the dead but for the new life they now have.

The Role of the Priest and Priestess in the Death Chamber

Whenever possible there should be a priest or priestess or at least some member(s) of the Initiate's own Order, Lodge, Coven or School in the death chamber. The strength and support of the Brethren of one's own Mother Lodge can be of great benefit not only to the dying but to the living. The Order may have its own rites and preparations which the passing member may wish to observe. The most immediate members of the family should be allowed to stay if they wish even if not members *providing this is the wish of the one passing, as theirs is the last word on the subject.* Try to be as unobtrusive as possible, prepare and go through the Rites with dignity and assurance. If by any chance the family are totally against the performance of the Rites and insist on their non observance despite the wishes of the departing, do not argue. Assure the one concerned that the Rites will take place in another place with a proxy, and then leave.

To do this, set up as near a copy as may be possible of the death chamber, or at least in a similar kind of bedroom. Ask another member of the Fraternity to stand proxy for the dying brother by standing at the head of the bed, and placing a photograph of the real person on the pillow. The proxy may then make answer for his/her brother.

Your robes should be plain with no show or display, simple, without lamens or insignia of rank, unless the Brother has asked that you be fully accoutred.

No more than five members should be present for each quarter and one to guide the Rite. If space is small, then four will suffice, one of whom may be the guide. If even this is too many then two is the smallest number. Remember it is a day to be joyful rather than gloomy and sad. Smile and try not to show your natural grief. Make sure you are clean: shower and wash your hair and put on clean underclothes before robing. Have everything you need to hand in a small case.

The Role of the Guardian of the Rite, and this may be either male or female, is to hold all parts of the Ritual together. They must organize, assemble and finally conduct the actual Rite. At the risk of upsetting the ladies I hold that this is better suited to the talents of the male Priest. His is the role of the

Pillar of Force, and Force is what is departing; he is needed to guide it and seal the way after it has passed. The role of the Priestess, with her greater insight on the inner levels, is to prepare the spirit and act as its Midwife through the process of birth into a new dimension. As the Pillar of Form she is needed to reassure the departed that it will still have a form after death.

You might say that these two roles are those of Mother and Father, for they fulfil the same roles as they do at each new birth. It is important to understand that death is a birth, just as birth is the beginning of death. The Priest needs strength and an ability to stabilize conditions both on the inner and outer levels. The Priestess needs to have endurance, understanding and the ability to love but to let go. She must be The Stabat Mater. Both of you are there to act as the physical counterpart of the Psychopompos of ancient times. It is an ancient and demanding role to take on, one that demands the best you have to offer.

All Schools, Orders and Fraternities should have a Rite of Passing and train their members in its usage, or maybe have a special team that specialize in such work. Members of that Order should regard it as a priority to attend a fellow member in extremis when they are called upon to do so.

Where the Old Religion is concerned, many covens and groups have their own ways of dealing with the death. The brunt of the Rite falls to the High Priestess, but that of the Lord should not be ignored, for it is he who takes away the spirit, either by means of the White Stag and shapeshifting, or as Herne with the Wild Hunt. In Part Three I shall offer several Rituals in different Traditions. Do not be afraid to rearrange them if you wish, they are not sacrosanct and I will not be offended if you do so. Take them and change them as you need, they are meant to be only a basis on which you may hang your own ideas.

The Modern Priesthood of Anubis

There is a growing need for a new kind of Occult Order – one with trained people who can perform the last office of all for those on the edge of passing into the Light. It is a fact that more and more people are dying physically alone and that is something that should not happen. Everyone needs the comfort of caring hands, soft voices and loving hearts. Nurses and doctors do their best, that is not denied, but all too often they are overworked and understaffed. They cannot spare the time that is needed to stay by a bedside for the many hours that it may take for someone to pass across.

In ancient times such priests could be called upon at any time. It was their particular work and they had trained for many years to understand just how to deal with the dying. It is time for such a priesthood to rise again.

Some schools and Orders are already beginning to think along such lines and to train selected men and women in the twin disciplines of Healing and Aid for the Dying. It is not simply a matter of sitting with the person but of 'spending time' with them, getting to know them, helping them to think back through their lives and building a 'death working' with them. It means having the time and the will to visit them time and again, indeed whenever it is needed, and being there at the end.

Some do have relatives, but they may be far away, unable to visit often, if at all. Some people are entirely alone and have need of comfort and reassurance, something they may have been without for a long time. Most of these people are not of an occult persuasion, and would not understand it, or even welcome it. Yet their needs should be met with an understanding of their ways and beliefs by a trained Watcher.

There are groups, schools and courses where such training can be obtained. One is run by The Buddhist Society and it is essential that some form of accepted training is undergone by those intent on taking up this work. A knowledge of the religious and ethnic procedures of different faiths is important so that no offence is given or religious taboo is breached.

It is work that can be hard to deal with emotionally as it is not just old people that die, but young people in the prime of life, mothers with children growing up and who are distraught at the idea of leaving them, fathers facing the prospect of leaving a young family to cope alone, and young children who cannot always understand what is happening. This special kind of work needs a very special kind of person, one with strength as well as love, endurance as well as gentleness. The overemotional and the sentimental are not for this work; ask yourself if you are able to watch people die without getting overemotional and still be able to help them with love and patience. Could you wait all night by a bed until the dawn releases the soul and then be able to face the day for yourself?

When helping and being with someone who is facing death, maybe several months away, sentimentality is not what is needed, but stark honesty and clearheadedness. Death is not romantic, it is harsh, unsightly and often painful to watch, yes, even the death of an Initiate. There will be times when all the occult knowledge in the world will not be enough to help a Lodge Brother or Sister in their extremis. You must be prepared for that and be able to accept it. Then the burden lies upon you, for you must work without their input, using your own strength.

What the Law Allows

Can you be buried anywhere you want? Well, yes and no. If you have a large amount of land and wish to be buried in a chosen spot, even though the land is yours you are up against two arguments. What if you or your heirs wish to sell the land at a later date? The new buyers may not like the idea of a burial plot as part of the deal. In the course of time the land may be put to a different use – building, for instance. If the headstone has gone for one reason or another it would be understandable if someone built a house over the remains. If a tree had been planted instead of a stone and that came down, you are in the same kind of predicament. You must have heard of foundations of an old house being dug up and remains found under them. Not all of them are the result of a long forgotten murder.

Contamination of Water

The second argument against burial on private ground is more serious. There is the actual lie of the land, the water table, sewers, underground streams, etc. All and any of these may be contaminated by the remains. You might well ask, what about cemeteries already in existence? In the old days when a graveyard grew about a church, nobody had thought about the possibility of contamination, yet it has always been there. Many an old graveyard has been built in a position where the local water must have become tainted at some time or another. The outbreaks of cholera, typhoid and other epidemic diseases during the past may well have been the result of such practices.

The point being made here is that if you wish to be buried on your own land, or on common land for that matter, you must seek advice and permission from the local authorities. They must investigate the circumstances and the area surrounding the place of your choice. If there is no likelihood of trouble, then if you are persistent you may get your way.

You may prefer to go about it in a different way and ask the local authorities if there is a piece of ground available for sale, where you can make arrangements to be interred. If you give them an idea of where you would like to be buried they may be able to accommodate you. And so long as people, tourists, walkers, hikers, etc are not going to fall over it, and care is taken to preserve and maintain it and prevent its desecration you may be lucky. For example, in the Channel Island of Jersey, high on a rocky slope looking out over the sea, lies the grave of Jesse Boot, the First Baron Trent of Nottingham. It is a quiet secluded place reached by a flight of stone steps and surrounded by high railings.

There are precedents. You can also arrange to be buried at sea if you wish, though it can be expensive. There are records of someone trying to have their body dropped into the crater of a live volcano. That one did not succeed.

Cremation

Ashes may be disposed of in almost anyway you wish. You can be scattered over a sacred site so long as it is not private ground, but a direct request to the owners may be successful. You can be sprinkled over the sea, dropped into a hole and a tree planted over you.

Can you have your funeral conducted as you wish? Yes, you can, but not, if you are thinking in terms of a pagan funeral, in a church belonging to either the Roman Catholic Church or the Church of England. The former will insist on the regular service, and the latter, while possibly giving in gracefully over unusual music and readings, will draw the line at a Priest or Priestess giving the blessing either to those gathered or over the coffin. A Unitarian church may accommodate you; they do in the USA in many States. In fact they have proved themselves to be helpful and understanding to those of the occult persuasion in that country. If not, then the chapel adjoining a Crematorium may be amenable. However, there is nothing to stop you once you have a place from arranging the service as you wish. You may ask a Priest or Priestess of any persuasion to take the 'service'. Whatever music you wish may be played and you may have speakers of your own choice. Perhaps the best way is to arrange a simple funeral and plan a more elaborate memorial service a month or so later.

The Last Message

One thing you might like to think of is the possibility of speaking to your family and friends at your own funeral or at the memorial service through the medium of a taped recording. You can record this at your leisure well ahead of time and perfect it until you get it right. You can give a brief message to certain people and tell them that you are happy to have shared a part of your life with them. A little joke or two will lift their sorrow and, as the old time comedian used to say, 'always leave 'em laughing'. Death is not the end of everything, it is the beginning of something else, an adventure, a new way of life, an exploration, a time to learn and strive to make it better the next time around. All this and more you can get across in a message.

1 *The Oxford Book of Mystical Verse*. Oxford University Press 1917 and subsequent editions.
2 See 'The Calling of a Soul' in *The Tree of Ecstasy* by Dolores Ashcroft-Nowicki. Published by Aquarian Press 1990.

9

License to Depart

For tho' from out our bourne of Time and Place
The flood may bear me far,
I hope to see my Pilot face to face,
When I have crost the Bar.
Alfred Lord Tennyson, 1809–92

The Rites of Departure

1 Egyptian

The Rites of Departure of any tradition may be conducted after death simply by using a proxy or while the Initiate is still alive and can make the responses. Therefore, although it may be regarded as akin to the Last Rites of other faiths, it may also be joined to the preparation of the body or, as a third alternative, it may be performed after interment with a photograph of the 'Osiris' placed on the altar. This equates with the practice in ancient Egypt of invoking the Kha into a statue or into the mummy of the deceased for the purpose of the Rite. Remember always that there are three great Rites of Passage: Birth with all the promise of a full and happy life before one; the Passing from Childhood into Adulthood; and Death with its balance held between the old and the new. Each has its true and proper Rites.

If the Initiate is still conscious and able to speak for him/herself, then make sure that you start the rite with his or her full consent. If it is performed after death has taken place or the person is too weak then someone must stand in for the 'Osiris' and speak for them. If the family is not of the Initiate's persuasion, then it is up to that person to specifically state that they wish the rite to be conducted. It will ease things considerably if the person makes their wishes known long before there is any need for the rite. It should be talked over with the family and if there is any resistance it must be dealt

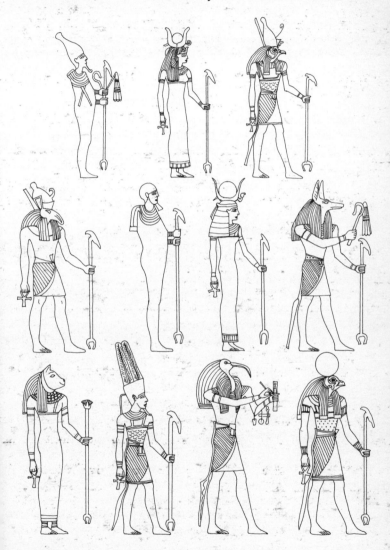

Figure 9.1 Procession of the Gods.
Top row: Osiris, Isis, Horus, Second row: Seth, Ptah, Hathor, Anubis. Bottom row: Bast, Amun, Thoth, Ra.

with then and not close to the moment of death when any controversy will only upset everyone concerned.

If the Initiate makes his/her wishes known strongly, then the family should in all decency allow the departing their wish. It can be made part of the will and its contents made known to the heirs if need be. Having said this some families will object anyway, even if the one most concerned has requested it. Everyone has the right to receive, prior to or just after death, their chosen way of making their peace and preparing themselves for the aftermath of death. No one should be intimidated into accepting what the relatives want for the sake of peace and quiet. Just as it is your life, so it is your death.

The ancient Egyptian burial rites were lengthy and obviously their time span is out of the question for us. However, I have prepared a much shortened version of the rite which runs roughly parallel with that of its ancient predecessor. Always bear in mind that the 'Osiris' is already in the process of death and should not be tired more than can be helped.

I have stipulated five people: four to act as supporters and one as the Guardian of the Rite, i.e. Anubis or, if preferred, as the Sem Priest. The idea of having five people equates with five being the number of Geburah and of the archangel Khamael who breaks down that which is no longer viable. If the family is sympathetic and wishes to stay it will be comforting to the 'Osiris', especially if they can act as the supporters. There is nothing more beautiful than sharing such a rite with one's close family.

You will need the following things for the ceremony: an Ankh drawn on parchment in gold ink; an Eye of Horus made in the same way; a bowl of warm, scented water; a towel; four pottery jars with lids which should be painted or drawn with the heads of the Four Sons of Horus (If this is not possible then just write the names. These are: Qebhsnuf, the Falcon-headed son; Duamutef, the Anubis-headed son; Hapi, the Ape-headed son; and Imsety the Human-headed son.); a censer of light incense; the 'Adze and the Ur-Hekau sceptre' (these must be made specially, see instructions at the end of the chapter); a large white handkerchief; seven different oils;[1] small phial of pure water; a small cup of wine and a portion of new bread; some honey and some salt. I have not used the

Figure 9.2 Anubis and the weighing scales.

idea of the 'Leg of the Bull Calf' or anything representing it. The idea of its use is not in keeping with our role as the Initiator of the Younger Brethren.

The priests/priestesses are robed in white, with either white slippers or white socks. If you have collars of the Egyptian type, then use them over the robes. If possible the Guardian of the Rite should wear an Anubis head mask. Clean nightwear is all that is needed for the 'Osiris' or, if strong enough, and it is preferred, then perhaps the usual Lodge Robe. The four assistant priests will take various forms as the rite progresses. At first they represent the Four Sons of Horus, the Guardians of the organs of the 'Osiris'. Later they stand for the Gods. Then they become the Assessors in the Hall of Judgement.

If possible the bed should be positioned so to give access all round. Two candles should be placed beyond the foot of the bed so that the 'Osiris' sees them as the Gates of the Duat. The Priests enter, each carrying one of the four jars. The Guardian enters with the incense. The rest of the required articles should be in position beforehand.

The Rite

After circling the room each priest sets down his jar beside him and, with the Guardian who stands at the head with the incense, begins the invocation.

First section
Priest: HAIL TO THEE OSIRIS, THOU WHO STANDS BEFORE THE GATES OF THE DUAT.
Others: PREPARE THOU THY KHA TO MAKE THE JOURNEY TO THE HALLS OF MAAT.
Osiris: ACCORDING TO THE LAWS MADE BY ATUM RA, I SHALL PREPARE.

Second Section
Priest: THOU ART HELD WITHIN THE ARMS OF NUIT, AND IN HER WOMB SHALL THY SPIRIT REST UNTIL REBIRTH.
Others: THE REALM OF LIGHT SHALL BE OPEN TO THEE, IN THE BOAT OF MILLIONS OF YEARS THOU SHALT BE SEATED.
Osiris: FROM NUIT I SHALL RETURN WHEN IT IS ORDAINED BY THE GODS.

Third Section
Priest: LET NOW THY SPIRIT REST IN THE HANDS OF ANUBIS THE GUIDE AND THE COMFORTER.
Others: ISIS AND NEPHTHYS SHALL SURROUND YOU WITH THEIR WINGS.
Osiris: I AM CONTENT THAT IT SHALL BE SO.
The Four Sons of Horus pick up their jars.
Hapi: (steps forward) UNDER MY PROTECTION, UNDER THE HAND OF HAPI SHALL I PLACE THE LUNGS OF . . . THE OSIRIS (places hand over chest wall and then over jar, replaces lid and steps back).
Duamutef: (steps forward) UNDER MY PROTECTION, UNDER THE HAND OF DUAMUTEF SHALL I PLACE THE STOMACH OF . . . THE OSIRIS (places hand over stomach, then over jar, replaces lid and steps back).
Qebhsnuf: (steps forward) UNDER MY PROTECTION, UNDER THE HAND OF QEBHSNUF SHALL I PLACE THE INTESTINES OF . . . THE OSIRIS (places hand on belly then over jar and replaces lid and steps back).

Imsety: (steps forward) UNDER MY PROTECTION, UNDER THE HAND OF IMSETY SHALL I PLACE THE LIVER OF . . . THE OSIRIS (places hand over liver, then over jar, replaces lid and steps back)

Priest: THUS AND THUS SHALL IT BE DONE ACCORDING TO THE WORD OF ANUBIS LORD OF EMBALMERS.

(The jars are placed at the head and foot and on each side of the bed. The priest now washes the face, hands and feet of the Osiris with the water and dries them gently.) I HAVE PREPARED THY BODY AND MADE IT FIT TO GO BEFORE THE GODS I NAME HAPI, DUAMUTEF, QEBHSNUF AND IMSETY, THE SONS OF HORUS AS THE GUARDIANS OF THY ENTRAILS. ART THOU SATISFIED OSIRIS OF . . .? IS THY HEART WELL WITHIN THEE?

Osiris: I AM SATISFIED AND THE HEART IS WELL WITHIN ME. LET THE SONS OF HORUS BE BLESSED IN THEIR SERVICE.

Priest: (takes censer and circles the Osiris four times) THOU ART PURE IN THY HEART O OSIRIS. THOU ART PURE IN THY MIND O OSIRIS. THOU ART PURE IN THY BODY O OSIRIS. THOU ART PURE IN MAAT O OSIRIS.

Others: IN ALL THINGS THOU ART PURE. WE, THE SONS OF HORUS, SAY THIS.

Osiris: IN MY HEART, MIND, BODY AND SOUL I AM PURE.

Priest: (takes rainwater and sprinkles it in drops over the Osiris in four separate offerings) THOU ART PURE, THE PURIFICATIONS OF HORUS ARE THY PROTECTION. THOU ART PURE, THE PURIFICATIONS OF SET ARE THY SHIELD. THOU ART PURE, THE PURIFICATIONS OF THOTH ARE AS A SWORD IN THY HAND. THOU ART PURE, THE PURIFICATIONS OF SOKAR GIVES THEE ENTRANCE TO THE HENU BOAT.

Others: THUS AND THUS IT IS DONE.

Osiris: THUS AM I PROTECTED, IT IS WELL WITH ME.

Priest: (takes censer and censes the head, the eyes, the nose, the mouth) PURE IS THE INCENSE THAT BLESSETH THE WISDOM OF OSIRIS, PURE IS THE ESSENCE THAT OPENETH THE EYES OF OSIRIS, PURE IS THE SCENT THAT ASSAILETH THE NOSTRILS OF OSIRIS, PURE IS THE SWEETNESS THAT SHALL PREPARE THE MOUTH OF

OSIRIS TO OPEN UNTO US.

Others: THUS AND THUS IT IS DONE.

Osiris: THE GODS ARE BLESSED FOR THIS.

Priest: (censes Eye of Horus and presents it to the Osiris) I HAVE PRESENTED UNTO THEE THE EYE OF HORUS AND THE ODOUR THEREOF COMETH UNTO THEE, IT MAKES THEE CLEAN, IT ADORNETH THEE, IT LIETH UPON THY HEART (puts Eye over heart).

Others: THUS AND THUS IT IS DONE.

Osiris: I WAS ASLEEP (dead) AND HORUS AWAKENED ME TO LEAD ME ON MY JOURNEY. I WAS DREAMING AND ANUBIS AWAKENED ME TO A NEW LIFE. THE LORD OF AMENTI IS MY FATHER, THE SUN HAWK AND THE JACKAL ARE MY BROTHERS. IN THE ISLAND OF KHEBIT SHALL I BE REBORN INTO THE LIGHT. LET ME BE IN TRUTH AN OSIRIS.

Priest: (to the four supporters) LET US MAKE THIS MAN/WOMAN LIKE UNTO OSIRIS THE SON OF GEB. LET US DEAL WITH HIM/HER AS DID SET WITH HIS BROTHER THAT HIS WISH BE FULFILLED (priest approaches the Osiris and touches his mouth with his little finger) O OSIRIS I EMBRACE THEE. (The supporters lay their hands upon the Osiris, doing this in memory of the smiting of the body of Osiris by his brother Set.)

Others: THUS AND THUS IT IS DONE.

Priest: (brings small piece of bread and offers it to the Osiris) I BRING UNTO THEE BREAD THAT IN AMENTI THOU SHALT HAVE LIFE. I CALL HORUS TO THEE.

First Supporter: (advances and offers small piece of bread and honey) I AM HORUS, IN THE NAME OF MY FATHER OSIRIS I OFFER THEE BREAD AND HONEY. I CALL MY MOTHER ISIS TO THEE.

Second Supporter: (advances and offers small piece of bread and salt) I AM ISIS, IN THE NAME OF OSIRIS I OFFER THEE BREAD AND SALT. I CALL MY SISTER NEPHTHYS TO THEE.

Third Supporter: (advances and offers sip of wine) I AM NEPHTHYS, IN THE NAME OF OSIRIS I OFFER THEE WINE. I CALL MY SON ANUBIS TO THEE.

Fourth Supporter: (advances, offers Ankh to nose of Osiris) I AM ANUBIS I OFFER TO THEE THE BREATH OF ETERNAL LIFE.

Priest: (brings the Adze and with it touches the eyes of the Osiris) BEHOLD I SHALL OPEN THY TWO EYES AND THOU SHALT SEE IN AMENTI. (touches ears) I SHALL OPEN THINE EARS AND THOU SHALT HEAR THE VOICES OF THE GODS. (touches mouth) I SHALL OPEN THY MOUTH FOR THEE AND THOU SHALT GIVE PRAISE TO THE LORD OF AMENTI.

Osiris: I SEE THE GLORY OF RA, I HEAR THE VOICES OF ISIS AND NEPHTHYS, AND TO THE LORD OF AMENTI I GIVE EVERLASTING PRAISE.

Priest: (Brings the Ur-Hekau wand and touches the mouth) THY MOUTH HAS BEEN MADE FIRM FOR THEE, NUIT HATH LIFTED UP THY HEAD, HORUS SHALL PLACE IN THY MOUTH SPELLS OF GREAT POWER. ANUBIS SHALL GUIDE THEE. THOU SHALT RISE UP AS KING OF THE SOUTH, AS KING OF THE NORTH, AS KING OF THE EAST, AND AS KING OF THE WEST. THOU ART OSIRIS AND THE GATES OF THE DUAT SHALL OPEN UNTO THEE. NOW THOU SHALT HAVE KNOWLEDGE OF THE WORDS OF POWER THAT OPEN THE GATES OF THE DUAT.

(The priest now anoints the Osiris with the seven oils. Over the face of the Osiris he places a large white (new) handkerchief. This is to prevent the mixture of oils burning the delicate skin of the face. The cloth should be kept wrapped and used as a face covering after death. The forehead, both ears, eyes, nostrils, mouth, hands and feet are anointed with each oil.)

Priest: WITH THE FIRST OIL I ANOINT THEE, THAT THOU COMEST SWEET SMELLING BEFORE THE GODS. ON THY HEAD AND EARS, ON THINE EYES AND THY NOSTRILS, ON THY MOUTH AND THY HANDS AND FEET I ANOINT THEE. WITH THE SECOND OIL I ANOINT THEE, THAT THOU SHALT OFFER SWEETNESS TO THE SONS OF HORUS THAT GO WITH THEE. WITH THE THIRD OIL I ANOINT THEE, THAT IN THE HALL OF THE ASSESSORS THOU SHALT NOT LACK COURTESY. WITH THE FOURTH OIL I ANOINT THEE, THAT THE LORD OF EMBALMERS SHALL KNOW THEE FOR HIS OWN. WITH THE FIFTH OIL I ANOINT THEE, THAT THY KHA SHALL STAY BY THEE ON THY JOURNEY THROUGH THE DUAT. WITH THE SIXTH OIL I ANOINT THEE, THAT THOSE

Figure 9.3 The Kha, spirit double of the body which dwelt in the tomb.

THAT GUARD THE WAY SHALL BOW BEFORE THEE. WITH THE SEVENTH OIL I ANOINT THEE, THAT ALL EVIL SHALL DEPART FROM THY PATH ON THE JOURNEY TO AMENTI. BEHOLD THOU ART COME TO THE HALL OF MAAT AND THERE SHALL THY HEART BE WEIGHED.

(Here each of the supporters shall speak the questions of the Forty Two Assessors in turn, and the Priest shall answer for the Osiris.)

1. HAST THOU CARED FOR THY BODY AS A GIFT OF GREAT WORTH?
2. HAST THOU LIVED THE FULL TIME ALLOTTED TO THEE?
3. HAST THOU BEEN CLEAN IN MIND AND BODY?
4. HAST THOU LOVED WITH THE BODY ONLY WHERE THE HEART IS ALSO?
5. HAST THOU HAD KNOWLEDGE OF THOSE FORBIDDEN THEE?
6. HAST THOU KEPT ONLY TO THE SWORD OR THE DISTAFF?

7. HAST THOU RESPECTED THE YOUNGER BRETHREN OF THE EARTH?
8. HAST THOU STOLEN?
9. HAST THOU TAKEN FOOD AND DRINK TO EXCESS?
10. HAST THOU KILLED?
11. HAST THOU SPOKEN UNJUSTLY OF ANOTHER?
12. HAST THOU BEEN ENVIOUS?
13. HAST THOU BEEN JEALOUS?
14. HAST THOU TOLD LIES?
15. HAST THOU BEEN LAZY?
16. HAST THOU PROFANED THE MYSTERIES?
17. HAST THOU BEEN PRIDEFUL?
18. HAST THOU STRAYED FROM THE PATH ORDAINED FOR THEE?
19. HAST THOU LUSTED FOR PRECIOUS METALS?
20. HAST THOU BEEN TOO WORLDLY?
21. HAST THOU BEEN JUST IN THY BUSINESS DEALINGS?
22. HAST THOU REPAID DEBTS AS QUICKLY AS POSSIBLE?
23. HAST THOU GIVEN TO THE NEEDY?
24. HAST THOU LIED TO GAIN FROM OTHERS?
25. HAST THOU USED LAUGHTER AS A WEAPON?
26. HAST THOU BEEN A FRIEND?
27. HAST THOU HATED ANOTHER TO THE EXCLUSION OF ALL ELSE?
28. HAST THOU LENT THY BODY TO DEMONS?
29. HAST THOU BEEN A JOY TO THY PARENTS?
30. HAST THOU HONOURED ALL FAITHS THAT ARE OF THE LIGHT?
31. HAST THOU TAKEN TIME TO BE AT PEACE WITH THE GODS?
32. HAST THOU REJECTED ADVICE GIVEN IN LOVE?
33. HAST THOU LISTENED TO THAT NOT MEANT FOR THINE EARS?
34. HAST THOU LIVED IN THY FAITH AND IN LIGHT?
35. HAST THOU PROTECTED THOSE WEAKER THAN THEE WHEN IT WAS NEEDED?
36. HAST THOU ENSLAVED ANOTHER?
37. HAST THOU FACED THE MIRROR OF SELF
38. HAST THOU TAKEN THE WORDS OF ANOTHER AS THINE OWN?

39. HAST THOU UNDERSTOOD THAT LIFE ENDS ONLY TO BEGIN?
40. HAST THOU REMEMBERED THE ANIMALS AND BEEN COMPASSIONATE TO THEM?
41. HAST THOU EVER WORKED MAN OR BEAST BEYOND ITS STRENGTH?
42. I AM THE LAST ASSESSOR BUT MINE IS THE QUESTION THAT CAN SET THEE FREE. IS THERE *ONE* UPON THE EARTH WHO IS GLAD THAT YOU WERE BORN?

Priest: I WILL ANSWER THAT QUESTION. I AM GLAD THAT . . . WAS BORN AND I WILL OFFER THAT ANSWER TO BE THE FEATHER OF TRUTH AGAINST WHICH THE HEART OF THIS OSIRIS WILL BE WEIGHED. DO YOU STAND READY TO BE JUDGED?

Osiris: I STAND READY.

Priest: THEN LET THE HEART BE WEIGHED. (now there should be silence for at least two full minutes) THE HEART IS PURE, THE SCALES OF MAAT ARE BALANCED, THE SOUL MAY GO ON.

Others: LET ALL WHO HEAR REJOICE.

All: OSIRIS, THY WAY IS CLEAR INTO AMENTI, THY MAAT VESTMENTS ARE OFFERED UP WITH THEE. THE GODS STAND UP BEFORE THEE, THEY STAND WITNESS TO THEE. RA LISTENS TO THY WORDS AND HORUS WALKS BESIDE THEE. THOU HAST ENTERED THE HALL OF JUDGEMENT AND COME FORTH AGAIN WITH A FACE LIKE UNTO THE SUN. THE COMPANY OF THE GODS IS PLEASED WITH THY PRESENCE. INTO THINE OWN PLACE ART THOU COME. PURE ART THOU, PURE ART THOU, PURE IS THE OSIRIS, PURE FOREVER.

The priest and supporters circle once and then depart.

See the illustrations for the shape and formation of the Adze and the Ur-Hekau sceptre. They can be made from wood or even from strong card and coloured accordingly.

2 Greek

This ritual requires the help of four women and one man. Again they should be Initiates or at the very least people who have a certain amount of experience in ritual and High Magic. The bed or the position of the person for whom the rite is

Figure 9.4a Osiris.   *Figure 9.4b* Thoth, the Recorder
                                         of Deeds.

being held should allow of free access all round. The priestess
takes on the role of Persephone, the Queen of the Dead, the
man that of Charon the Ferryman, while the other three
women are the Fates.

You will need: a cup of pure water; a small cup of wine; a

silver coin; a ball of thick thread (or better still if you can obtain it, a ball of hand spun wool or cotton thread); a wooden spindle; a sharp knife; incense of fresh aromatic herbs (Rosemary, Lavender, Tansy or Amaranth, Rue, Pine, Dittany, Thyme, and just a little Sage); plain white robes for the women. Persephone should wear a dark blue or green veil over the face, above a coronet of fresh flowers. She should have a small basket of flower petals and leaves. For Charon a darker robe with a hood. As in the previous rite, this may be performed by proxy either before or after death has taken place. The term 'Shade' is used here to designate the departing soul.

The Three Fates sit to one side, one spins the thread, one winds it into a ball as it is spun and the last waits with the knife. Charon takes his stand at the head of the bed or behind the chair and waits to be called. Persephone lights the incense and with it she circles the room beginning in the East and pausing at the four quarters.

Persephone: (East) THIS IS THE PLACE WHERE MEET THE SKY AND THE EARTH. THIS IS THE PLACE OF APOLLO

Figure 9.5 Greek mourners going to the tomb.

THE GOD OF LIGHT AND OF HEALING. (sprinkles petals)
HERE WAS THE POINT OF THE SHADE'S BIRTH, WHERE
THE NEW SUN OF LIFE WAS KINDLED AND THE
THREAD WAS FIRST SPUN. APOLLO, LORD OF LIGHT,
SON OF ZEUS, LOOK UPON THIS SHADE WHO LONGS
FOR PEACE AND FOR THE GREAT AND FINAL HEALING
THAT IS IN THY GIFT. GRANT LEAVE FOR A PLACE IN
THY CHARIOT AS IT CLIMBS INTO THE HEAVENS.

Shade: LORD OF LIGHT, SON OF LETO, GRANT ME
PEACE AND THE FINAL HEALING, IN THY GRACE AND
STRENGTH LIFT ME INTO THY CHARIOT THAT I MAY
RIDE WITH THEE TO THE SETTING OF THE SUN.

Clotho, First Fate: I IT WAS WHO BEGAN THE THREAD OF
THY LIFE, AND I HOLD THE SPINDLE STILL, NOT YET
HAS THY LIFE RUN OUT. A STRONG THREAD, A LONG
THREAD, AND I WILL PREPARE ANOTHER THREAD FOR
THEE WHEN THOU SHALT COME AGAIN ON EARTH.

Shade: I BLESS THEE FOR THIS THREAD OF LIFE AND
FOR ITS STRENGTH NOW PAST.

Persephone: (South) THIS IS THE PLACE OF NOON AND
THE PRIME OF THE SHADE'S LIFE. THIS IS THE PLACE
OF ARES (APHRODITE) GOD(DESS) OF STRENGTH,
LOVE AND FULFILMENT. THESE WERE THE YEARS OF
DELIGHT AND JOY AND YOUR ACHIEVEMENT, A TIME
WHEN THE THREAD WAS STRONG AND SURE ON THE
LOOM OF THY DAYS (sprinkles petals) ARES/APHRODITE
LOOKS UPON THE SHADE THAT NOW PREPARES TO
LEAVE THE SUN OF EARTH THAT IT MAY LOOK UPON
THE HIDDEN SUN BEYOND. GRANT STRENGTH AND
JOY IN THE NEW LIFE TO BE.

Shade: LORD OF STRENGTH/LADY OF LOVE AND
BEAUTY, GRANT ME PEACE AND JOY IN THE LAND
BEYOND THE STYX. WELCOME ME WHEN I SHALL
RETURN.

Lachesis, Second Fate: I HAVE SPUN THE THREAD OF LIFE
FOR THEE THROUGHOUT THE YEARS. GOLD AND
SILVER, SORROW AND LAUGHTER, JOYS AND TEARS
HAVE I GIVEN TO THEE. NOW THE THREAD GROWS
THIN AND SOON IT WILL BE CUT BY MY SISTER. FEAR
NOT, ANOTHER THREAD WILL BE PREPARED FOR THEE
AND THOU SHALT COME AGAIN AND MANY TIMES
AGAIN, FOR SO IT IS FOR HUMANITY.

Shade: I BLESS THEE FOR THY CAREFUL SPINNING AND FOR THIS PRESENT THREAD NOW DESTINED TO PART.

Persephone: (West) THIS IS THE PLACE OF THE SUN'S SETTING AND THE ENDING OF LIFE. THIS IS THE PLACE OF HADES, LORD OF ELYSIUM AND OF THOSE DREAMS THAT COMFORT THE NEWLY DEAD. GENTLE IS MY LORD AND STRONG. HIS ARMS WILL BEAR YOU FROM THIS EARTH AND INTO A TIME OF REST. FEAR HIM NOT. (sprinkles petals) THE FINAL YEARS HAVE BEEN ALLOTTED THEE AND NOW THEIR TIME HAS RUN. HADES, LORD OF QUIET DREAMS, LOOK UPON THE SHADE THAT NOW LOOKS TO THEE FOR COMFORT. GRANT A GENTLE RELEASE INTO MY CARE.

Shade: LORD OF DREAMS, COME SWIFTLY THAT I MAY REST BENEATH THY CLOAK OF SOFT NIGHT, STAR ENTWINED. CALL THY SERVANT CHARON TO TAKE ME ACROSS THE DEEP DARK RIVER.

Atropos, Third Fate: A FEW MOMENTS MORE AND I SHALL CUT THE CORD OF LIFE FOR THIS TIME. CURSE ME NOT FOR THIS IS THY DESTINY, AYE AND MANY TIMES SHALL I DO THIS FOR THEE.

Shade: I CURSE THEE NOT, BUT BLESS THEE AND MY DESTINY LAID IN THY HANDS.

Persephone: (North) THIS IS THE PLACE OF DEPARTURE, THIS IS MY OWN PLACE, THE PLACE OF DREAD PERSEPHONE. (raises veil and throws it off) YET I AM NOT FEARFUL TO LOOK UPON NOR TO SPEAK WITH FACE TO FACE. THIS PLACE IS BUT THE GATEWAY TO MORE LIFE. (sprinkles petals) COME SHARE WINE WITH ME. (brings cup of wine and drinks from it, then offers to Shade) TAKE THOU THIS COIN TO PAY THE FERRYMAN, AND ANOTHER TO PAY FOR ONE WHO HAS NO MEANS OF PAYMENT, AND IN DOING THIS THOU SHALL BE BLESSED BY THAT SPIRIT. (places two coins in the hand of the Shade) NOW SHALL I CALL UPON CHARON TO MAKE READY HIS BOAT. (goes to foot of bed) CHARON, FERRYMAN OF THE STYX, COME FORTH AND SHOW THY FACE TO PERSEPHONE, THY QUEEN.

(Charon comes forward and stands beside her.)

Charon: I AM AMONG THE MOST ANCIENT OF GODS. SINCE THE FIRST MAN AND WOMAN DIED I HAVE

FERRIED THEIR SOULS ACROSS THE WATERS OF FORGETFULNESS. I HAVE MANY NAMES AND YET I AM ALWAYS THE SAME. ALL SHALL SIT IN MY BOAT AT THE APPOINTED TIME AND TAKE THAT LAST JOURNEY INTO THE HALLS BEHIND SUN. FEAR ME NOT FOR I AM THE HELPER, THE GUIDE, THE COLLECTOR OF SOULS. TELL ME THY NAME SHADE, THAT I MAY CALL IT ACROSS THE STYX AND HERALD THY COMING.

Shade: I WAS KNOWN IN THIS LAST LIFE AS . . . I CALL THEE FRIEND AND HELPER. ACCEPT FROM ME THIS COIN IN PAYMENT, AND ANOTHER FOR ONE WHO HAS NO PAYMENT. I KNOW THEE, THOU ART HERMES, AND ANUBIS, THOU ART THE LORD OF ANNWN, THOU ART THE GENTLE GUIDE OF DEATH. WILLINGLY I GO WITH THEE. BRING ME THE CUP OF FORGETFULNESS, FROM THE WELL OF LETHE. (Charon brings the cup of water and help the Shade to drink) GATHER ABOUT ME AND BLESS ME AS I LEAVE. ATROPOS, LAST OF THE FATES, CUT THE CORD AND LET ME GO ON INTO THE HALLS BEHIND THE SUN.

Atropos: IT IS CUT (cuts thread) GO FORTH BRAVE SOUL AND COME AGAIN IN TIME.

Persephone: THE LAST GIFT OF ALL IS THE KISS OF PERSEPHONE (kisses Shade) AND SO REST AND SLEEP. THE GODS THEMSELVES WEEP FOR THEE.

The Fates leave quietly, then Persephone, finally Charon who should change and then go to walk in a quiet place, if at all possible crossing water at some point. If this is not possible then let him step over a bowl of water as he crosses the threshold. At he walks he should imagine that the Shade walks with him and finally is met by the *real* Charon and taken onwards. Then he may return. The coins should be placed with the Shade when the body is prepared, the petals swept up and scattered over a quiet place, the two cups emptied and *broken*, and the shards buried.

3 Celtic

Today when the word Celtic is heard it is often used to describe an intermingling of several quite different aspects of a once-central theme. Modern Neo-Paganism has taken certain areas and adapted them for its own use. This is not to decry the practice, anything that will help the survival of a tradition should be considered helpful. Change is always with us; it is not possible for any of the mystery traditions to say they have remained totally unchanged. They have all been decimated through long ages of neglect and persecution. What is left to us we must nurture as best we can and hope that we are doing things as near to the original as we can get.

The name Celt takes in a very wide geographical area embracing as it does the Irish, the Scots, the Welsh, some areas of England and, of course, the Celts of Brittany. But that does not even begin to cover it, as careful study shows that the Celts have even wider links that run throughout Europe and on into what is now Turkey and beyond.

This means that the tradition we are now left with is what we might euphemistically call a Celtic Stew. Long forgotten essences of a thousand tribes, customs, traditions and behaviour patterns are entwined into a richness that continues to thwart attempts to unravel it past a certain point. But perhaps if we stopped trying and allowed the 'scent' of the stew to arouse old racial memories we might come a little nearer to the truth. There are currently in Britain three people who have come close to that truth: John and Caitlín Matthews and Bob Stewart. All are writers, Caitlín and Bob are also musicians, and John is one of the few people I would classify as a true mystic. For all of them the Celtic Tradition is a way of life.

With so much 'in the stew pot' as it were, it becomes very difficult to pick out enough of one ingredient to make a comprehensive whole. Much better then to select a few features that are relative to the whole and use them as imaginatively as possible. There are some areas in which all the Celtic traditions meet: music and poetry is one (the Celtic love of words is legendary); their reverence for the symbol of The Head is another, and for the last I have taken their love of the sea in all its forms and moods and incorporated it into the legend of the glass death boat. Yes, I know there are many more, too many to bring together within one short ritual so for now, these must suffice to give the rite its essence of Celtia.

For those wishing to make use of this particular death rite the most important ingredient of all is the Death Mask which stands in lieu of the Sacred Head. This needs to be made well in advance by the person who will use it. Take your time and make it as well and as true to life as you can. To make such a mask needs time and patience, qualities that are not easy to find when one's time grows short, which is why it should be made ahead of time. You will find that the making of such a Sacred and important symbol becomes a Death Path in itself, taking time, effort, and determination.

To make the mask, grease the face well and place over it a piece of fine cotton that has been soaked and then well wrung out: a large handkerchief will do. Gently press the cotton into the crevices of the face. If you can find it, old fashioned buckram is even better since that can be soaked and pressed onto the face, making two holes for the nose, and allowed to harden as it dries out. This impression can then be used as a base on which to mould the actual mask. This may be done with either papier maché or with strips of bandage soaked in plaster of Paris, applied gently and pressed into place to make a fair image of the person. If you have the time and the patience you can make a mould of the face and, with one of the plastic resins now available for model making, fashion a less fragile mask. Or you may like to try something called Gypsona, a plaster-impregnated bandage used in hospitals to make casts for broken limbs. However, this heats up as it dries and may be uncomfortable to use. Once made to your liking, and it may take several attempts, the mask may be left as it is, or sprayed either gold or silver with perhaps Celtic spirals of blue paint on the forehead and cheeks. Alternatively, you might paint the face light blue and use a darker hue for the decorative circles.

On the inside of the mask write your given name and, if you should wish to do so, your mystery name and perhaps the name of your Lodge or Order. Now you need to write your Death Song or Poem. This is not as hard as it seems, it can be as long or as short as you wish. It should contain elements of your life, its most joyous and its saddest times. It should tell something of what you have achieved, what you feel you might have done better. It can contain a hymn or invocation to one of the Gods or Goddesses and perhaps words of comfort for those you will leave behind. If you feel you have little skill in writing an actual poem, then write it as an essay upon your life, or even as a letter. The very act of writing such a thing will make you reflect upon your life and recall the events of which you write.

Make two copies of the material, seal one into an envelope and place with someone you trust. Give instructions that it is to be read aloud at the appropriate time. The other copy should be taped to the inside of the mask.

Now you must take some beeswax, about the size of a golf ball (you can render down a small beeswax candle for this). Make it soft and pliable and form it into a ball, press into it some head and body hair, a nail paring and some spittle, if you wish to do things properly, then add semen or vaginal fluids, thus making the wax the carrier of a small part of one's vital essence. This should now be pressed securely into the mask, in the hollow formed by the nose. You now have within the mask a part of *you*, your life, your achievements, your sorrows, your joys, your thoughts, your hopes and your fears. It also contains a part of the physical you that will link the two together. Pad the mask with tissue or soft cloth to keep the shape and either glue or tape it to a strong card backing. This seals it, keeping the contents together and safe.

Now frame the mask artistically with anything that takes your fancy. It may be silvered leaves, scalloped pieces fashioned from gold or silver coloured paper doilies, feathers collected from seashore and forest, dried flowers for a woman or a plait of nylon hair arranged in a Celtic style. It can now be covered with cling film, placed in a plastic bag and sealed until its time comes. Then, if preferred, fresh flowers, Holly and Berries or perhaps Ivy can be used to surround it – in the case of the latter it will give it the appearance of a Celtic Green Man.

This mask now represents the dead person, using the symbol of The Sacred Head as the means of carrying the soul across the sea to the island of Hy Brasil, sometimes known as Avalon, The Apple Isle, or St Brendan's Isle. Because it is a likeness and carries in that likeness an actual part of the person, i.e. hair, nail paring and spittle, it represents that person and may be treated as such.

Now we turn our attention to the 'boat' which will carry the Head. If you have the skill in carpentry then certainly make a properly shaped boat of light wood. If not, then a simple wooden board on which the mask may be glued or bound will suffice. It should be varnished on one side and around the edges, the underside should have the name, just the name, of the person written or painted on it. On the topside the

name of the 'boat' should be painted and maybe an eye to
guide it on its way.

When the boat is finished, affix the mask with its surround
firmly to the wood. You can now complete the Death Boat in
one of two ways. The first will make it into a 'glass' boat, which
will need mirror fragments. Get a new mirror and do *not* look
into it. Put it into a plastic bag and give it a few sharp taps
to break the glass into small pieces. Carefully glue these all
over the wood, wherever there is room. When the time comes
to use it, it will gleam and glisten and catch the sun and reflect
it back to those watching. You might like, instead of laying the
mask flat, to fix it so that it becomes a 'sail', the mask facing
out to the sea and taking the boat along the path of the setting
sun.

Or, if you prefer to use the mask in the Nordic Tradition,
you might block it out with straw, add a miniature sword
either bought in a model shop or made yourself. Add to this
a model of a dog and a horse and perhaps some small
personal belonging. This can be fired and set on the sea with
an appropriate invocation to the Gods.

When your mask and boat have been made, hallow and
dedicate them with salt and water, incense, and a drop of wine
on its lips. Then pack them away until such time as they are
needed. Arrange with a member of your Lodge or Order for
the short ritual of the Mask to be performed *after* your death.
If you are to be cremated then the mask may be used to cover
a small container of ashes instead of the padding already
suggested.

The Rite of Departure

This ritual is in the form of a blessing and a thanksgiving for
the life that is now ending. Music is an important part of it
and is played throughout the rite itself. The Celtic Harp is the
preferred instrument but any music that is favoured by the
departing is good. It should not be overloud but provide a
background to the ritual.

The person should be, if possible, propped up into a near
sitting position with a red cloak or blanket spread over the
bed. On the feet a pair of light sandals are placed. These may
be made from a pair of inner soles bound on with ribbons.
On their right side place a sword if it is a man, a spindle and
thread if it is a woman. On the left place a round stone

ornamented with a spiral pattern for both men and women.
On the head a circlet of green ribbon should be bound about
the temples.

You will also need a large piece of card painted with a spiral
pattern that is in fact a maze with the path leading clearly into
the middle. This symbolizes the road into the Underworld,
where the encounter with the Lord of Annwn takes place, and
then the road leading out and into the Land of the Ever Young.

The officiants are three women representing: Danu, an
aspect of the Mother Goddess of the Celts; Brigid, originally
a Fire/Warrior Goddess; and Annis the Old Wise One. Also
one man to represent Arawn, the Lord of the Underworld.
Each woman holds a symbol to be used in the rite. Danu has
an apple (cut a thin segment that can be easily detached, for
eating), Brigid carries a small chalice of wine, and Annis a cup
of water with a little lime or lemon juice in it to represent the
Bitter Herb.

The Rite of the Mask
If possible this ritual should take place on the third day after
death, it can however be done at a later date as it may take
time to make arrangements to travel to the nearest seashore.
It should always be carried out on the ebbtide so that the wave
action carries the boat out to sea.

Make sure that the mask is secure, and place a small candle
of the nightlight type on the boat. A short nail sent through
the wood from the underside will provide a point on which
to fix the candle firmly.

When you arrive at the departure point for the Death Boat,
spend a little time quietly remembering the person and
thanking them in your heart and mind for all that they have
meant to you.As the sun sinks down, one person who has
been chosen either by the departed one or from among those
gathered steps forward and reads the poem, essay or letter,
a copy of which is already 'on board' the boat. Then some
music should be played as the short ritual proceeds. I would
suggest music of the Celtic Harp as this is the most suitable.
Alan Stivell is perhaps the best known but there are others.
Bob Stewart's Psaltery music is another good choice. Keep the
music going until the boat can be seen no more.

The Rite
Draw a circle on the sand and place the boat within it. The officiant should sprinkle it with salt.

Officiant: THOU ART THE LIKENESS OF . . . MADE BY HIS/HER OWN HANDS AND CARRYING THE ESSENCE OF . . . I SPRINKLE THEE WITH SALT TO CLEANSE AWAY ALL TRACES OF SIN, AND TO BLESS THEE WITH THE SUBSTANCE OF THE EARTH (sprinkles with water) I BATHE THEE WITH WATER AND BID THEE SHED NO TEARS FOR THOSE YOU LEAVE BEHIND, BUT TO PLACE YOURSELF UNDER THE PROTECTION OF THE MOON AS YOU SET SAIL FOR THE SACRED ISLE.

All: MAY THE TRIPLE MOTHER TAKE YOU UNDER HER CARE, MAY SHE SMILE ON YOU THROUGHOUT YOUR JOURNEY. MAY THE DAGDA STRIKE YOU WITH HIS STAFF AND BRING YOU TO LIFE ONCE MORE.

Officiant: I PUT BREAD AND HONEY UPON YOUR MOUTH THAT YOU MAY BE SUSTAINED UPON YOUR JOURNEY TO THE APPLE ISLE. (puts piece of bread dipped in honey on mouth of the mask) I GIVE YOU WINE TO SLAKE YOUR THIRST AS YOU SAIL INTO THE WEST. (drips wine on mouth of mask)

All: MAY LUGH THE GOD OF LIGHT BE YOUR GUIDE, MAY BRIGID THE FIRE MAID WARM YOU, MAY LLYR THE SON OF THE WAVE LEND YOU HIS HORSES TO DRAW YOU TO THE WEST.

Officiant: I LIGHT THE TORCH THAT WILL GUIDE YOU. (lights candle) WE BID YOU FAREWELL . . . WE GIVE THANKS FOR THE LIFE YOU LIVED AMONG US, WE PRAISE THE GODS THAT BROUGHT US TOGETHER. WE ASK THAT YOU BE THERE TO GIVE US WELCOME WHEN WE TAKE THE SAME ROAD INTO THE SETTING SUN. LET US MAKE OUR PRIVATE FAREWELLS. (each person circles the boat in silence and bows to the mask)

Officiant: LET US SET FREE THE SPIRIT OF . . .

The boat is picked up and taken to the water. It is best if its bearers wade out far enough for the sea to take it straight out into the ocean. Sometimes it might be best if it is set upon the sea from a rock point further out, or even if possible laid on the water from a boat. Everyone casts flowers, leaves, or paper boats carrying messages of love into the water. Small foil cake cases carrying nightlights make a simple but beautiful picture if they are strung together and tacked to the edge of the Death Boat. They can be seen for a long way as they sail along the path made by the last rays of the sun. Wait, watch, and remember the person until the sun has fully set, or until you can see the lights no more.

This is not as elaborate as other rites, but then the actual making of the mask is itself the major part of the ritual.

Below I offer a kind of template for a Death Song or Poem, its contents can be altered to suit other circumstances, places and events. It is meant purely as a pattern, though not the only pattern. You might look to early medieval poetry for other examples.

Song of Return

The sea was my cradle from my day of birth,
Her songs have filled my soul since then, unceasingly.
Not a warrior my father, but a man of thought and
    passion,
In my mother he found a depth of spirit that matched his
    own.
Words and Music were my wet nurses filling heart and
    soul,
Love was my lullaby and dreams of far shores filled my
    days.
Of companions I had but few,
But one four footed held my heart
My night dreams were filled with visions of other suns and
The night sky was a longed-for country with the Moon my
    lighthouse.
Summers were filled with the songs of bees and warm
    sunshine.
Until one man's evil smashed my summer dreams and sent
    me
Homeless and fearful into a darker night than any I had
    known.
Manmade lightning and swift death walked my streets,
Friends left without word
Travelling to the shore that now awaits me.
Long years of exile unendurable, longing for my sun-kissed
    isle
Filled all my mind, yet other dreams were forming, calling
As from far away beyond the gates of birth to another time
    and place.

The inner eye was opened and painful memories peeped
     through,
Awareness of other lands not of earth became known to
     me,
Destiny was born with me
And in her footsteps I followed duty bound.
False hopes, false loves and dark despair became my
     teachers
And in another island I sought to find that other part of
     me that I had lost.
Dark days and darker nights, tears and loneliness
     unbearable was my lot
Until it was decreed my time of test over and with
     another's hand
In mine I struggled now to relearn teachings long forgotten.
Back through time to the echoing Halls of On
I heard my sandals whisper on the ancient stones.
Time passes and I grow in strength, two children grace my
     life in joy.
Now came a teacher from the past, the work began, the
     knowledge to unfold.
Step by painful step I learned what I had learned before,
Seeking to remember lore once known and used and now
     so far away.
A moment in time silence on a busy street, strange incense
     on the air.
A standing figure and a new awakening, an old love
     returned.
A heart too full to cry, the spirit yearning speaks, 'I know
     you well'
The beloved is with me once again
For this I was born and nothing else.
Year builds on year and all too soon my youth had gone
     into the past
Yet wisdom and deeper happiness grew that I might share
     all this.
Under my hand it grows, each name a building stone
     etched upon the mind.
Once, long ago I knew a place like this, cool courtyards
     and quiet rooms.
Softly spoken words to eager ears sharing knowledge and
     understanding.
Childish visions come full circle, here in Alexandria was
     my farthest shore.
Again I teach as I have done before
And will again until time shall end.
Now it is done, life passed and I wait upon the coming of
     the Night.

I hear the muffled sound of oars beating the water, the
    death boat comes.
One last look on faces dearer to me than life, one press of
    the hand.
The setting sun waits not and I must go beyond it to the
    golden land.
I shall come again as it is so decreed and we shall meet
    again
Clasp hands and hold each other close.
The boat is here, but the shore is empty.

This is a lightning sketch of a lifetime meant to fit the cadence
of the spoken voice, but it is merely an offered pattern to the
reader.

4   Neo-Pagan

I have always thought that it would be far nicer to take that
last breath outside on a warm summer's evening, or in a sun-
filled garden during that mysterious time we call high noon,
when the angels change guard in heaven. Then, some years
ago, I came into contact with an elderly woman, now alas no
more, who in her youth had belonged to a group whose
tradition was certainly pagan, and very old in origin. From her
I learned that in the past, in the early years of the century, they
had always held a Death Feast in the outside for those who
were close to passing. Only if it was bitterly cold or the
weather completely intemperate did this not occur and some
actually closed their eyes for the last time 'in the greenwood',
with a great fire blazing amid a celebration feast and with
people all around them, honouring the one departing as if he
or she were already of the Gods. Time and again the cups of
wine would be raised in salute, and messages to loved ones
already on the farthest shore were given to the departing
guest to deliver, and gifts were given in both directions.

   That part of the person's regalia that was to be passed on
would be given at the Death Feast, as well as small token gifts
of china, jewellery, pictures, books and much treasured trifles.
These were handed over and received with great delight,
especially by the younger ones. Gifts for the one taking the
last journey might include a handmade robe of white
handwoven linen to be used as a burial shift, every stitch
therein being placed by hand. If it was a woman it would have
been embroidered with flowers of every colour, and every

woman in the group would have had a hand in the work. If a man, the decoration would have included tiny bunches of Grapes, Ivy leaves and Holly. An Athame, usually handwrought, was given for either sex and placed between the hands at burial. A silk waist cord and a pair of canvas shoes with their 'wood' name stitched on the front were also given, the latter to make the long journey to the Land of the Goddess more comfortable. There were gifts of wine and food for the Feast itself and the whole evening became a celebration for the person whose Death Feast it was.

Then, with this marvellous ceremony of leave-taking fresh in their minds and hearts they would be taken back home and, within a few days or even hours, had taken the Low Road. This kind of ceremony left everyone feeling uplifted rather than weepy and morose and, as the old lady said, one had the feeling that it was just a sort of retirement dinner and one would see them again shortly.

Wonderful as it sounds, it is hardly practical in urban areas, or in any but the most isolated places, but something similar can be done by cutting the Celebration of Death into two distinct parts. The Death Feast itself takes place during the last few weeks of the person concerned and was arranged according to their strength and ability to take part. A ritual of Farewell is offered and the traditional gifts exchanged. Then a later ceremony after the burial or cremation.

For the first you will simply need to prepare as if for a party. It is important to invite the people who are important to the person the Death Feast is for and *not* those important to *you*. This is purely and simply for the one who is taking the Low Road. Decide how many they feel able to cope with and for how long. If they can get up then clear one room of excess furniture and provide just seating and tables. Decorate it as if for a birthday, for it *is* a new birth into a different life.

I would suggest that alcohol be reduced to simply red and white wine with no spirits (no pun intended), with fruit and biscuits, small cakes, sandwiches, the usual party fare and a special cake. This is an opportunity for everyone to say goodbye and give thanks for the blessing of one person's life and love.

In the days before, help the person to choose and wrap small gifts from among their treasures to be given out to people. Arrange a large comfortable chair with cushions and a rug in case they get chilled and make that the point of focus in the room. If they are bedridden, then arrange the party in a nearby room and decorate both rooms, leaving the door open so that people can come and go without too many being in at the same time.

A nice touch would be to set out some personal photographs for people to look at, and have some that can be given away so everyone will have a likeness of them to take away. Remember these rites are for those who do not see death as others see it, they are Initiates, students, priests, and priestesses of the ancient mysteries and traditions. For such people as these, death is an adventure, they will not be phased by the idea of a party to celebrate their death.

If it is possible the gift of a handmade robe in white, green, blue or whatever colour they might prefer, should be made. Every person should have been given the opportunity to add a few stitches. This is a labour of love and as such will wrap the outworn body with great power on its last journey. In addition each person could bring a small packet of incense or sweet smelling herbs to be scattered over the body after it has been prepared and clothed. Lavender, Thyme, Rue, Rosemary, Pine and maybe, if in season, some small pine cones as a symbol of the fertility that will one day bring them to new birth.

The Rite of Farewell should not be over long as the emotional content may be too much for both the person concerned and those attending. People should be told at what time the rite is to be performed and given time to change into their robes. If everyone is robed it adds to the occasion.

A small table is placed in the centre of the room, The High Priestess and the Lord of the Forest take their places in the North, the person for whom the rite is intended sits in the West with two people beside them. One is to speak for them in case emotion overcomes them, and the other is to perform those tasks that will need to be done. The Maiden takes the East and the Mother the South. (To explain the reasons for the above to those not familiar with this tradition, the North is seen as the place of greatest power, the West as the place of the Spirit, the Maiden being 'new and untouched' stands at the place of new light, the Mother or Lady stands in the South, having known the fire of love and the knowledge of birth.

On the table are a chalice of wine, a plate of bread and honey, salt and water in separate containers, a lighted candle, a small glass of wine and a feather. The robe to be given should be lying on the table folded, and the incenses and herbs in a bowl also on the table. The Maiden holds a bowl of flower petals, the Mother holds incense. The Lord of the Forest holds the Sword. The Priestess is power in herself and needs nothing other than that.

Priestess: (takes salt and consecrates it) CREATURE OF EARTH, BY THE ELEMENT THAT RULES THEE I CASTE OUT FROM THEE ALL THAT IS BASE AND EVIL, AND I MAKE THEE PURE AND HOLY. CREATURE OF WATER, BY THE MOON THAT RULES THEE I CAST OUT FROM THEE ALL THAT IS BASE AND EVIL AND I MAKE THEE PURE AND HOLY. IN THE NAME OF THE GODDESS, I MAKE THIS SO. (She takes a small amount of salt, not all, and puts it in with the water.)

All: SO MOTE IT BE AS THE GODDESS WILLS.

(Priestess now circles the room casting the mingled salt and water before her, cleansing the room. A circle of Light should be visualized.)

Priestess: WITH SALT AND WATER I CLEANSE THIS PLACE AND MAKE IT SACRED FOR OUR RITE. LET THE GODDESS MAKE THIS PLACE HER OWN AND KEEP IT PURE. (she returns to her place)

All: SO MOTE IT BE AS THE GODDESS WILLS.

Priestess: LORD OF THE FOREST, WITH THE SWORD DRAW THOU THE SACRED CIRCLE ABOUT AND WITH THY STRENGTH PROTECT THE GODDESS AND HER PEOPLE.

(Forest Lord circles the room dragging the point of the sword on the floor to form a circle. This should be visualized as a circle of fire.)

Lord: WITH THE SWORD OF POWER I ENCIRCLE THIS PLACE TO PROTECT THOSE WITHIN IT FROM ALL EVIL AND HARM. I CLAIM THIS PLACE FOR THE GODDESS. (returns)

All: SO MOTE IT BE AS THE GODDESS WILLS.

Priestess: MAIDEN, WITH YOUR FLOWERS BLESS AND HALLOW THIS PLACE AND MAKE IT SWEET FOR THE GODDESS AND HER PEOPLE.

(Maiden circles the room casting her petals as she goes. A circle of many colours should be visualized.)

Maiden: WITH THE BEAUTY OF EARTH I ENCIRCLE THIS PLACE THAT IT MAY BE A PLACE OF FRAGRANCE AND COLOUR FOR THE GODDESS AND HER PEOPLE. (returns)

All: SO MOTE IT BE AS THE GODDESS WILLS.

Priestess: LADY AND MOTHER, WITH SWEET INCENSE MAKE YOUR OFFERING TO THE GODDESS AS A GIFT FROM HER PEOPLE.

(Lady circles the room with the incense, and the smoke should be visualized as a wall between the outside world and the now hallowed place.)

Lady: WITH SWEET SMELLING INCENSE I MAKE THIS OFFERING TO THE GODDESS ON BEHALF OF HER PEOPLE HERE GATHERED. WE BEG THY PRESENCE O GODDESS.

All: SO MOTE IT BE AS THE GODDESS WILLS.

Priestess: THOU WHO SITTEST IN THE PLACE OF THE WEST, WHO PREPARES TO JOURNEY TO THE MOTHER OF US ALL, WHAT IS THE TASK YOU LAY UPON US THIS NIGHT?

West: I WOULD ASK THAT THE DOORS OF THE WEST ARE OPENED TO ME, THAT I MAY PASS THROUGH AND BEGIN MY JOURNEY TO THE SACRED ISLE OF THE GODDESS. I WOULD GIVE THANKS FOR MY LIFE AND FOR ALL THAT IT HAS CONTAINED, BOTH THE SORROWS AND THE JOYS. I GIVE THANKS FOR MY BIRTH AND I GIVE THANKS FOR THE DEATH THAT NOW FACES ME, FOR I BELIEVE THAT IT WILL HOLD A NEW LIFE THAT WILL BE LIVED IN THE LIGHT OF BEAUTY THAT IS THE FACE OF THE GREAT MOTHER.

Priestess: LET US INVOKE THE GREAT GODDESS, MOTHER OF US ALL.

All: (turn to North) GODDESS OF THE CORN, GIVER OF BREAD, WE INVOKE THEE TO THIS PLACE BUILT WITH POWER. WE GIVE THANKS FOR THE LIFE OF . . . AND ASK THY BLESSING UPON THIS THY CHILD. (turn to East) GODDESS OF THE RAINBOW, BRINGER TO BIRTH, WE INVOKE TO THIS PLACE BUILT WITH POWER. WE GIVE THANKS FOR THE LIFE OF . . . AND ASK THY BLESSING UPON THIS THY CHILD. (turn to South) GODDESS OF

FIRE AND PASSION, LADY OF BEAUTY, WE INVOKE THEE
TO THIS PLACE BUILT WITH STRENGTH AND LOVE. WE
GIVE THANKS FOR THE LIFE OF . . . AND ASK THY
BLESSING UPON THIS THY CHILD. (turn to West)
GODDESS OF THE WATERS, BRINGER OF THE SLEEP OF
DEATH, WE INVOKE THEE TO THIS PLACE BUILT WITH
DREAMS. WE GIVE THANKS FOR THE LIFE OF . . . AND
ASK THY BLESSING UPON THIS THY CHILD. SO MOTE
IT BE AS THE GODDESS WILLS.

Priestess: I SHALL PREPARE THE CUP OF DEPARTURE
AND BLESS THE ROBE. (She goes to the altar and asks the
Maiden and the Lady to unfold the robe and hold it over the
altar. She then blesses it with salt and water, censes it, and
passes the candle over and under it three times. Then the robe
is folded and given to the West by the Maiden. The Priestess
takes the small glass of wine, into this she puts a pinch of salt.)
INTO THE WINE I PUT THE BITTERNESS OF TEARS, THE
ELEMENT OF EARTH. (puts drop of water into glass) INTO
THE WINE I POUR THE ESSENCE OF THE SPIRIT, THE
ELEMENT OF WATER. (douses the candle flame in the wine)
IN THE WINE I DOUSE THE FLAME OF LIFE, THE
ELEMENT OF FIRE. (stirs wine with the feather and breathes
on it) WITH THE FEATHER OF THE WING I STIR THE WINE
AND ADD THE BREATH OF MY MOUTH IN BLESSING.
THIS IS THE ELEMENT OF AIR. (Holds up the glass for all
to see) GODDESS OF EARTH AND WATER, FIRE AND AIR,
BLESS THIS WINE AND THE ONE WHO DRINKS IT.
SMOOTHE THE WAY FOR THEIR FEET UPON THE PATH
THAT LIES BETWEEN THE GATES OF THE WEST. (She
takes it to each person in turn, they place their hand over it
and say a blessing of their own making. The Priestess takes
it all round then finally comes to the West where the glass is
offered for the West to drink. It must all be drunk – if
preferred the 'wine' can be fruit juice – the Priestess kneels
and asks for a blessing from the West, then in turn, the Forest
Lord, the Maiden, and the Lady. If it is not too tiring then each
person in turn may come to be blessed and in doing so to
make their farewells.)

Priestess: LET US CLOSE THE RITE.

(She circles the opposite way sprinkling the salt and water
as before.)

I WASH AWAY THE CIRCLE OF CLEANSING AND

RETURN THIS PLACE TO THE PHYSICAL PLANE ONCE
MORE.

(The Forest Lord does the same with the sword.)

Lord: I CALL BACK THE CIRCLE OF PROTECTION SET
UP, AND RETURN THIS PLACE TO THE PHYSICAL PLANE
ONCE MORE.

(The Maiden circles the room with her bowl of petals.)

Maiden: I CALL BACK THE CIRCLE OF COLOUR AND
FRAGRANCE AND RETURN THIS PLACE TO THE
PHYSICAL PLANE ONCE MORE.

(The Lady circles with incense again in the opposite
direction.)

Lady: I PUT OUT THE CIRCLE OF FIRE I LAID ABOUT
THIS PLACE AND RETURN THIS SACRED GROVE TO THE
PHYSICAL PLANE ONCE MORE.

All: SO MOTE IT BE THIS DAY AS THE GODDESS WILLS.

Priestess: THE RITE OF DEPARTURE IS ENDED.

All file out and this should end the evening. Remember that
the farewell you have made is a spiritual and ritual one and
it will hold even though you may of course see some of the
people again.

The second part of the Rite is performed after death has
taken place. If the deceased has been cremated the ashes can
be the centre piece. If they have been interred a lock of hair
should be taken immediately after death for use in this ritual.

A secluded place must be found where a small fire can be
safely lit (make sure you have permission if this is needed).
A few days before, gather some small logs of any sweet
smelling wood. Apple, pear, some sandal and cedar shavings,
pine, juniper, anything that has a pleasant scent when
burning. The ground should be cleared down to bare earth,
or some bricks may be laid down and the logs built up on
them. Pour some scented oils over the logs, lavender,
rosemary, juniper, sandal, and sprinkle with herbs and
spices. If there are ashes, these should be sprinkled over the
logs, if not then a wooden box containing the hair should be
placed at the centre of the fire.

An invocation to the Goddess and the Forest Lord then
follows, and the fire is lit. As it burns each person in turn
comes forward and throws some incense on to the flames and
speaks of their love and feeling for the departed friend. Then

as it burns low a period of meditation on the person being honoured is observed. Finally, when the fire is quite out, the ashes may be given to the winds, to the earth, or to the sea. The final 'gift of remembrance' should be a small bell, or a string of temple bells placed high up in a tree in a place where they used to walk or to which they were very attached.

5 Qabalistic

A ritual of departure can be easily put together in this tradition by using the Angelic, Devic and Elemental invocations offered in Chapter Seven. Used either separately or as a continuous ritual it will form a powerful invocation to those forces of Light. An Initiate may also use the Tree of Life as a Ladder of Withdrawal by meditating on each sphere of the Tree, beginning with Malkuth and aligning each one with an area of his/her life. By gradually moving up through the Tree you will find the sphere of Da'ath becomes the leaping-off point, beyond that you will go beyond the Gates of the West and come at last to safe harbour. Keep this in mind if, as may be the case, your time should come when you are alone and without the support of your Lodge brethren. The times in which we live are dangerous and erratic, and we have no choice as to the where, when and how.

---

1 Rosemary, myrrh, cedar, sandal, frankincense/kyphi, lotus and olibanum.

10

Earth, Water, Fire and Air

I arise today through the strength of heaven;
Light of sun. Radiance of moon,
Splendour of fire. Speed of lightning.
Swiftness of wind. Depth of sea.
Stability of Earth. Firmness of Rock.
The Breastplate of St Patrick

Returning to the Four Elements

All human beings are a wonderful combination of the four
elements. They live in and through us, just as we exist
physically because they work together. We are over 90% water,
we have the trace elements that are of the earth in our bodies,
we breathe a mixture of gases that feeds our bloodstream and
keeps our brains fed, we have a central core of body heat that
regulates itself according to our environment. We could not be
closer to the elements than we already are. Because we are so
closely entwined they become affected by the way in which
we use or misuse our bodies. If we smoke, the element of air
is fouled and polluted, if we drink too much alcohol the liquid
content of our bodies damages the liver, if we do not eat
properly, or if we eat unclean or infected food, we do not get
the nutrients or minerals we need and sicken, if we lie in the
sun for too long day after day or work in industries where
intense light is used the over exposure to light and heat can
cause skin cancer.

   The brain is the tool, the mind is the foreman who uses the
tool, the spirit is the managing director, the body is the factory,
the elements making up the body are the workforce. Damage

the workforce and everything else functions on a lesser scale and may even run down to the point where the factory may close down. Drugs, alcohol, cigarettes, stress, wrong eating habits can affect not only us as people, but those elementals that make up our bodies.

At physical death all 'contracts' become null and void, the elements return to their own level. This being so it seems ungrateful to let them go without so much as a thank you or a simple blessing for the work and support given throughout that person's life.

The body may be disposed of in many ways, interment allows the body to return to the earth those nutrients that belong to it, quite literally 'dust to dust'. Cremation acts like a cleanser and reduces the body to ashes through the application of the fire element. Burial at sea returns the physical shell to its primeval womb of the sea (by the way it is possible for anyone to be buried at sea if they so wish, it can in fact be cheaper than buying an expensive burial plot). The Parsee religion exposes its dead to the air in open-ended Towers of Silence, where the body is left to disintegrate. The method you choose is up to you, but a ceremony of blessing for the Four Elements that served the body and kept it going for so long means that their existence is recognized.

This Rite concerns mostly those left behind, but if the Calling of the Elemental Kings is performed before death, then an extra blessing on the elements of the body may be invoked by the departing spirit. Do not forget to bless the body itself, it has some small sentience of its own and should not be left to face its disintegration alone. The placing of a Guardian as a companion for the body until it has fully disintegrated is a courtesy.

The actual rite is performed by four people who may be chosen by the deceased in advance. It will require four locks of hair to act as links with the person and the physical body. It can be performed in a Lodge/Temple or simply in a quiet room. If may also take place in the open where it is quiet and remote from the rest of the world.

In a lodge or indoors you will need an altar/table covered with a white cloth. On this place four paper napkins, or squares of felt or cloth at the four quarters in Blue, Red, Green, and Gold. On each square stands a symbol of the quarter: a censer of burning incense for the East; a lighted candle for the

South; a bowl of water for the West; and a bowl of mixed seeds and earth for the North. If you can get corn or wheat it would be even better, for as a symbol of resurrection it is unsurpassed. In the centre, stand a small altar light and a bowl of consecrated water mixed with a little wine, with a bunch of herbs with which to sprinkle it.

Robes should be worn unless you are working outdoors when a simple ribbon of the appropriate colour placed around the neck will suffice. The four locks of hair should each be tied with a thread of colour matching one of the quarters and placed on a small cloth, or you might like to use one of the small sarcophagi sold at the British Museum. There are several kinds and they make excellent holders for such things. Each quarter officer can, if it is wished, wear a surtout or tabard of the quarter's colours over their robe.

Begin with an invocation to the Archangel Metatron:

East: ANGEL OF THE PRESENCE WHOSE VERY NAME CONTAINS THAT WHICH IS, OF ITSELF, UNKNOWABLE, ALLOW US INTO THY RADIANCE FOR THE TIME OF THIS RITE. GIVE US SPACE WITHIN THY BEING FOR ONE SMALL MOMENT OF TIME. AND GIVE US LEAVE TO SPEAK.

South: ANGEL OF THE HIGHEST REALMS, THOU WHO HAST WALKED THE EARTH AS A MAN, THOU FOR WHOM THE GLORY OF THE HEAVENS WAS OPENED, GIVE THOSE GATHERED HERE IN THIS SACRED PLACE LEAVE TO SPEAK.

West: ELIJAH WAS THY NAME AND THE HAND OF THE CREATOR LIFTED THEE ABOVE ALL OTHERS. RENAMED AND CLOTHED IN THE RAYS OF THE SUN, METATRON, MIGHTY ARCHANGEL OF THE MOST HIGH, GIVE US LEAVE TO SPEAK.

North: IN THE DAYS OF THY LIFE, YOU WALKED WITH MEN AND WOMEN AND DID EAT AND SPEAK AND LIVE WITH THEM. AS THEY WERE, SO WE ARE, IN THY SPLENDOUR FORGET IT NOT AND GIVE US LEAVE TO SPEAK.

East: HEAR NOW THE WORDS OF THE EAST, IN THE NAME OF THAT WHICH CREATED THIS COSMOS AND SO ARRANGED THE LAWS THAT BIND IT. I CALL TO THIS PLACE THE BEING CALLED PARALDA, ELEMENTAL

KING OF AIR. IN PEACE AND LOVE I CALL THEE AND
SET THEE BESIDE ME AT MY RIGHT HAND. LORD OF THE
WINDS, TAKE THY PLACE IN THE EAST UNDER THE
BANNER OF RAPHAEL, REGENT OF AIR. BE WELCOME,
BE THRICE WELCOME. (turns to East and bows three times)
  South: HEAR NOW THE WORDS OF THE SOUTH. IN THE
NAME OF THAT WHICH CAME OUT OF THE
UNMANIFEST AND CREATED WITHIN ITSELF A MIGHTY
UNIVERSE, I CALL TO THIS PLACE THE BEING CALLED
DJINN, ELEMENTAL KING OF FIRE. IN PEACE AND LOVE
I CALL THEE AND SET THEE BESIDE ME ON MY RIGHT
HAND. LORD OF THE SECRET FLAME TAKE THY PLACE
IN THE SOUTH BENEATH THE BANNER OF MICHAEL,
REGENT OF FIRE. BE WELCOME, BE THRICE WELCOME.
(bows three times to South)
  West: HEAR NOW THE WORDS OF THE WEST. IN THE
NAME OF THAT WHICH SACRIFICED ITSELF TO CREATE
LIFE AND BRING HOLINESS INTO MANIFESTATION, I
CALL TO THIS PLACE NIXSA, ELEMENTAL KING OF
WATER. IN PEACE AND LOVE I CALL THEE AND SET
THEE BESIDE ME ON MY RIGHT HAND. LORD OF THE
OCEANS, TAKE THY PLACE IN THE WEST BENEATH THE
BANNER OF GABRIEL, REGENT OF WATER. BE WEL-
COME, BE THRICE WELCOME. (bows three times to West)
  North: HEAR NOW THE WORDS OF THE NORTH. IN
THE NAME OF THAT WHICH OUT OF THE DUST
CREATED HUMANITY AND GAVE IT BREATH I CALL TO
THIS PLACE GHOB, ELEMENTAL KING OF EARTH. IN
PEACE AND LOVE I CALL THEE AND SET THEE BESIDE
ME ON MY RIGHT HAND. LORD OF THE DEEP CAVERNS
TAKE THY PLACE IN THE NORTH BENEATH THE
BANNER OF URIEL, REGENT OF EARTH. BE WELCOME,
BE THRICE WELCOME. (bows three times to the North)
  (East now opens the box and each one takes out the piece
of hair tied with the colour of the quarter and places it on the
altar before them.)
  East: I CALL ALL HERE SEEN AND UNSEEN TO
WITNESS THAT THESE ARE TOKENS OF . . . WHO HAS
NOW RETURNED TO THE HIGHER REALMS OF LIGHT. IT
WAS THE DESIRE OF . . . THAT THOSE ELEMENTAL
BEINGS THAT SUSTAINED THE EARTHLY BODY RECEIVE
A BLESSING FOR THEIR WORK DURING THE LIFE OF

A BLESSING FOR THEIR WORK DURING THE LIFE OF THE BODY NOW RELEASED THEREFORE IN THE NAME OF . . . AND BEFORE THOSE PRESENT I CALL THE ELEMENTS OF AIR TO COME BEFORE THE EASTERN SIDE OF THE ALTAR AND THERE TO RECEIVE THEIR JUST DUES AND THEIR BLESSING. (All turn to face the East and bow, wait a few minutes and visualize the sylphs crowding about the altar. The Eastern officer takes the bowl of water and sprinkles it about the eastern section.)

AS I HAVE PROMISED, IN THE NAME OF . . ., SINCE TAKEN INTO THE LIGHT, I, . . ., PRIEST/TESS OF THE EAST, DO NOW OFFER TO THE SYLPHS OF THE AIR A BLESSING TO THE AMOUNT THAT THOU ART ABLE TO RECEIVE. BE BLESSED IN THE NAME OF THE ONE WHOSE BREATH YOU SUSTAINED IN LIFE. PEACE BE BETWEEN US, BE BLESSED, BE BLESSED, BE BLESSED. (bows, returns bowl to altar)

(All turn now to the South and bow. The officer takes the bowl and sprinkles water about the southern section.)

South: IN THE NAME OF . . . AND BEFORE THOSE PRESENT I CALL THE SALAMANDERS TO COME BEFORE THE SOUTHERN SIDE OF THE ALTAR TO RECEIVE THEIR JUST DUES AND BLESSING. AS I HAVE PROMISED, IN THE NAME OF . . ., SINCE TAKEN INTO THE LIGHT, I, . . . PRIEST/ESS OF THE SOUTH DO NOW OFFER TO THE SALAMANDERS OF FIRE A BLESSING TO THE AMOUNT THAT THOU ART ABLE TO RECEIVE. BE BLESSED IN THE NAME OF THE ONE WHOSE BODY YOU SUSTAINED IN LIFE. PEACE BE BETWEEN US, BE BLESSED, BE BLESSED, BE BLESSED. (bows returns bowl to altar)

(All now turn to the West and bow. The officer takes the bowl and sprinkles the western section.)

West: IN THE NAME OF . . . AND BEFORE THOSE PRESENT I CALL THE UNDINES TO COME BEFORE THE WESTERN SIDE OF THE ALTAR TO RECEIVE THEIR JUST DUES AND BLESSING. AS I HAVE PROMISED, IN THE NAME OF . . ., SINCE TAKEN INTO THE LIGHT, I, . . ., PRIEST/TESS OF THE WEST, DO NOW OFFER TO THE UNDINES OF WATER A BLESSING TO THE AMOUNT THOU ART ABLE TO RECEIVE. BE BLESSED IN THE NAME OF THE ONE WHOSE BODY YOU SUSTAINED IN LIFE. PEACE BE BETWEEN US, BE BLESSED, BE BLESSED, BE

BLESSED. (bows, returns bowl to altar)

(All now turn to the North and bow. The officer takes the bowl and sprinkles water over the northern side.)

North: IN THE NAME OF . . . AND BEFORE THOSE PRESENT I CALL THE GNOMES TO COME BEFORE THE NORTHERN SIDE OF THE ALTAR TO RECEIVE THEIR JUST DUES AND BLESSING. AS I HAVE PROMISED IN THE NAME OF . . ., SINCE TAKEN INTO THE LIGHT, I, . . ., PRIEST/ESS OF THE NORTH, DO NOW OFFER TO THE GNOMES A BLESSING TO THE AMOUNT THOU ART ABLE TO RECEIVE. BE BLESSED IN THE NAME OF THE ONE WHOSE BODY YOU SUSTAINED IN LIFE. PEACE BE BETWEEN US BE BLESSED, BE BLESSED, BE BLESSED. (bows and returns bowl to the altar)

(East now picks up the lock of hair with blue thread and blesses it in his/her own words. Each quarter follows in turn.)

East: OUR TASK IS DONE, OUR PROMISE FULFILLED, LET THIS SACRED PLACE BE CLOSED. (turns to East, hand outstretched) BY THE POWER VESTED IN ME I BLESS ALL WHO STAND IN THE EAST, RETURN TO THINE OWN PLACE IN LOVE AND GRACE.

FIAT, FIAT, FIAT.

South: (turns to South, hand outstretched) BY THE POWER VESTED IN ME I BLESS ALL WHO STAND IN THE SOUTH, RETURN TO THINE OWN PLACE IN LOVE AND GRACE.

West: (turns to West, hand outstretched) BY THE POWER VESTED IN ME I BLESS ALL WHO STAND IN THE WEST, RETURN TO THINE OWN PLACE IN LOVE AND GRACE.

North: (turns to North, hand outstretched) BY THE POWER VESTED IN ME I BLESS ALL WHO STAND IN THE NORTH, RETURN TO THINE OWN PLACE IN LOVE AND GRACE.

(East unties thread from hair and if outdoors allows the wind to take it away. If indoors it should be placed in a cloth until it can be taken and allowed to fly free in the wind.

South takes hair and holds it to the Flame of the Southern candle until it has burnt away.

West places hair in chalice of water and when the rite is done, will spill it all into the nearest body of flowing water.

North mixes hair with seeds and will take them to be scattered on fertile earth.)

East: FAREWELL . . ., UNTIL WE MEET AGAIN.

All: FAREWELL UNTIL WE MEET AGAIN.

East: THE RITE IS DONE. LET US DEPART IN PEACE.

11

Consumatum Est

I strove with none for none was worth my strife.
Nature I loved and next to Nature, Art.
I warm'd both hands before the fire of life;
It sinks, and I am ready to depart.
Walter Savage Landor, 1775–1864

The Memorial Rites

A celebration for the life of someone well loved is quite commonplace these days, and it seems a fitting way to say thank you to the spirit of such people. They are by no means dark and gloomy ceremonies but full of light and smiles as people share their memories of a mutual friend or relative.

Often such a ceremony is a means of contact for those who could not get to see their loved ones before they died. It also helps those who could not get to the funeral because of time, distance or for financial reasons to share their time of mourning with others, or to express their feelings about the person.

To be effective there should be a lapse of time before arranging such a ceremony, something in the order of a couple of months. This gives time to those who are most attached to get over the worst of their bereavement. It also allows time for arrangements to be made, people to be contacted and a location to be chosen.

For those concerned with the Christian Qabalistic tradition an orthodox church willing to allow such a ceremony should not be hard to find. However, when it comes to the more occult traditions this may prove more difficult. In the USA many Unitarian churches are working with occult groups, especially Wiccans, and sharing their premises with them. This is a wonderful caring attitude and one hopes the same open mindedness will make an appearance in the UK as soon as possible. The Quakers have a long history of opening their hearts and minds to other traditions and they have many places up and down the country where such a ceremony might be held. Make sure, however, that there is provision for music as I find that this more than any other part of a memorial rite lifts the heart and spirit.

There are a surprising number of ordained ministers willing to offer prayers and well chosen speeches for these occasions, even for occult groups. A Lodge/Order may wish to have its own priest or priestess conduct the ceremony and again, there is no law against this. A large hall such as those in one of the universities would be ideal and can be arranged outside of term times.

The person for whom the memorial is being held may have left instructions for such a meeting, or at least expressed certain wishes. These should be paramount when you are planning the whole thing. The family must be at the heart of the consultation. They may or may not be of the same persuasion in which case you may find that they will arrange something more to their liking and purely for themselves. There is still nothing to prevent friends and brethren arranging their own memorial service. Just be discreet and try not to upset the family.

Make sure invitations to attend are sent out well in advance, especially to those attending from overseas or from long distances away. Do not have too many speakers, three is the maximum. No matter how loved the person was, three hours in a draughty hall in either freezing cold or high summer can dim the memory pretty quickly.

Arrange the seating with the first few rows for family, special friends and those who worked closely with the deceased. Those who will be speaking should be seated in the first row of seats. Similar to a wedding, ushers drawn from friends and brethren will ease the worries of late comers or those looking for friends to sit by. If there is a Banner or a Device used by the person, then it should be displayed to advantage. If the speakers were of the same Order and they wish to use them, they should be allowed to wear their robes. There is usually a small room where they can change.

The hall should be made to look as nice as possible and if flowers are too expensive they can easily be augmented by greenery. It may be that the person belonged to several Orders or Lodges or had been made an honorary member. They may wish to send representatives, or they may come en masse. If so, keep them together in one area of the hall. In this way the Inner Level Guardians and Teachers are also ranged together.

While the people are still, arriving music is very important. Few occultists would choose hymns if given the chance, but there may be something they really liked. See that you obtain a good organist, there is nothing worse than a mediocre one. If you know someone who plays the Celtic harp they might agree to play while the congregation are taking their seats. Someone with a good voice, and like the organist it has to be good, might like to sing something soft and mood inducing.

Remember also that if you choose anything modern it is important that you inquire about performing rights. There may be a small fee to pay if you include anything composed or sung by a living artist. The copyright holders or recording studios are the people to ask. So now we come to choice.

You should count on at the very least twenty minutes of music as people arrive, maybe two pieces during the service, and two or three as they leave. This is quite a lot of music when you come to decide on it, but a good organist may be able to provide you with a list.

If you have no harpist you might think of getting permission to play a recording of one of Alan Stivell's collections. Again remember that you *must* get permission, as it is illegal to use a record or tape at a gathering without this, such a meeting constituting a performance in law.

Music I would suggest includes:

The Intermezzo From *Cavelleria Rusticana*.

Meditation From Thais.

The Humming Chorus from *Madame Butterfly*.

Interlude 'Going Home' From Dvorzak's *New World Symphony*.

Fingal's Cave by Mendelsson.

Pavane Pour un Enfant Defunte by Ravel. (This might seems a strange choice but the melody, though solemn, is not inharmonious with such an occasion.)

Solemn Melody by William Walton.

All these will provide you with good 'entry' music. You might
wish to have some sort of procession at the beginning of the
service, in which case I would suggest Waltons *Crown Imperial*
coronation march, but time it beforehand as it might need
cutting or lengthening.

Now you can begin the service with the officiant declaring
the 'intent' of the service. In other words saying something
like,

MY FRIENDS, WE HAVE COME TOGETHER IN JOY
TODAY TO CELEBRATE THE LIFE OF . . . AND TO GIVE
THANKS FOR THAT LIFE WHICH BEGAN ON (give date of
birth) AND ENDED ON THE PHYSICAL LEVEL ONLY ON
(give date of death) THIS IS NOT AN OCCASION OF
SORROW BUT ONE OF HAPPINESS AS WE LOOK BACK
ON THE TIMES WE HAVE ALL SHARED WITH . . .

And so on and so forth. This might last about ten minutes.

At this point you should introduce something different, a
five minute meditation on the person we are honouring and
remembering might be nice, or some soft music, maybe with
a piece of well chosen poetry which, well spoken with the
music as a background, can be very potent stuff. Now comes
the first guest speaker. Make sure your speakers confer with
each other well before time so they don't both tell the same
stories or quote the same instances. Nothing is worse than
waiting to make a speech only to find the speaker before you
is giving a carbon copy of the one you are holding in your
hand.

Allow each speaker ten minutes maximum, otherwise you
will be there all day. As it is, if you have been keeping to the
outline you are by now some twenty to twenty-five minutes
into the service already. It is at this point that you might
introduce the voice of the person themselves, either speaking
a personal message specially recorded ahead of time for just
such an occasion, or something they may have recorded, a
piece of a lecture for instance. This brings the person right into
the hall with you and makes them seem very real and close.

Now you can bring on your second speaker. A good tip is
to have one speak of the person's work, another about their
family/personal life, and if you are planning a third speaker,
you might use something about their achievements. After the
second speaker you need another piece of music, preferably
something light, just so long as it is not 'Amazing Grace'!

Might I suggest 'Memories' from *Cats* which is a lovely haunting melody with words that very appropriately end with 'Look, a new day has begun . . .' Or you might think in terms of a pathworking, even more effective if already recorded by the person concerned. This might take the form of a walk through a wood with the person speaking about the things you have all shared and ending with them saying 'well, this is as far as you can go, now I must go on alone, but we will meet again, look for me . . .'

If you must have a hymn, now is the time for it, something you can get your teeth into and let rip with your emotions. Finally you end with a blessing and a farewell from the officiant and then some stirring music from the organist as your congregation moves out of the hall. One hour from start to finish is what you should aim for, and allowing ten to fifteen minutes for people to get seated at the beginning and more or less the same to get them out at the end. Don't forget the programmes – many people keep them as mementos, so they should have the name date of birth and death, perhaps a black and white photo, and some appropriate quotation or piece of prose.

Handing over Robes and Regalia

It has been a part of some traditions that all regalia belonging to an Initiate should be destroyed on their death. In the same way all Temple furnishings such as altar, banners, hangings, and symbols, etc should likewise be destroyed if that Temple/Lodge/Order ceases to exist. However, in our modern world such things are very expensive to make, buy and build. Cheap labour and materials such as were available at the time of the Golden Dawn no longer exist. Therefore it may be time to re-examine this tradition and ask ourselves if it is necessary to destroy things that are often very beautiful and have taken time, effort and thought to create.

Robes are very personal things, and if they are kept as they should they become magical tools in themselves. Often as they are taken from their place of concealment the scent of past rituals is released, bringing memories with it. But robes of silk and velvet and brocade are not cheap to buy, sometimes running well over £100 for one robe. Such articles should not, in my opinion, be destroyed but handed on as personal gifts either to one's successor, or to one who will use and treasure them. They then become talismanic and help to inspire the recipients to greater effort in their magical work. This applies to capes, headdresses and ceremonial tabards.

In may be that an Initiate will wish to be buried in a favourite robe, though for my part I think that a plain black or white robe, perhaps with a simple cloak, is all that is needed. Choose carefully the person to whom such things are given. Stipulate that they are to be used as you have used them and not kept as museum pieces around which some ridiculous notion of 'guruship' might be built. Before they are handed over wear them to perform some small rite and as you do so, deconsecrate them so that your power, built up over many years is diffused. The next person to wear them must build up their own power with which to infuse them.

Lamens, which are hung about the neck, come in many shapes, forms and sizes. Some are simple, made of felt such as the first Rose Cross Lamen I ever made. It is still used and carries with it an aura of youthful enthusiasm. Others may be of silver or gold, wood or other metals, but made sacred by their use in many rituals. If it is something that carries authority of succession, then it should be handed on, as it is. Such a piece builds up power as it is passed from generation to generation. Less powerful items may be cleansed by their owner and then handed on to friends and companions for them to use and remember you in that use.

Magical Rings are difficult; they carry with them enormous personal links built as their power is from deep within the psyche. If you are lucky enough to have a son or daughter who intends to follow you into the Mysteries, then it may be given to them but only to wear when they have reached a time in their training when they can cope with it. A simple ritual of power containment with a password given to a trusted friend is the answer. When they judge the holder of the ring worthy of its power, then the password may be given to them.

A wand is something that, like a ring, can be extremely personal. An Initiate may have several, but will probably use one more than the others. This should go with them at either interment or cremation.

Swords likewise carry a tremendous personal charge, and personally I think the best way to deal with them is either to present them (after deconsecration) to the Temple or Order to be used perhaps in the Initiation ceremony only, or as a simple decoration, or to deconsecrate them and then break them and bury them in some isolated location giving them into the keeping of Ghob and the elementals of the earth. Bury them deeply. Personally I have never consecrated a sword to my own use, if I must use one I use one belonging to the Order itself.

Athames, used in the tradition of the Craft are sometimes handed down in a family where it is an ongoing religion from generation to generation. I have handled such things with their owners' permission and there is a tremendous sense of living power cached within them.

Chalices again are magical tools that are often given as a gift, indeed it is traditional that a personal Cup is received as a gift of love. This being so, they are the easiest to pass on with the same love and affection with which they came to you. But as with all these things, choose the receiver wisely and after much thought.

A Staff is often a far more potent magical tool than a wand. My own was something I had to wait many years to obtain because my requirements were unusual. It is for me more important that any other piece of equipment. It carries in its magnetic field everything I have learned, thought about, written, or dreamed of throughout my magical years. I have already selected the person who will receive it and have built into it a gradual release of power that will help her in the years to come.

All other magical tools, such as Thuribles, Candlesticks and altar pieces may be safely handed on to others or given to the Temple/Order for general usage. These are things that can be handed over well before death because if you have learned your craft well, you will no longer need them. When it all comes down to basics, they are just tools, props. I have often told my own students that any magician worth his or her salt can work magic stark naked in a desert with just their hands as Sword, Wand, Chalice and Platter.

The Instruction of the Soul

As you get older and, if wise, begin to plan for death, you need to set aside some time each day to think about what you may want to do during your time of rest, learning and preparation for the next incarnation. Does this seems strange? Why? You prepare for other things, so why not your existence after death and your next life?

During the time you have set aside take a long hard look at your life, your achievements and your character. Look for your good and bad points. See where you have succeeded and where you have failed. Ask yourself if you have been happy in the work you do everyday, if there is something you have always wanted to do or to be? Now is the time to start planning for your next life by seeding ideas, first into the present personality, then sending the information higher into the Individuality with instructions for it to be taken up into the Primal spark. Far fetched? Not at all, any good 'boss' will listen to what the worker on the line has to say. You live each life to learn more and to grow in wisdom and understanding, therefore it is up to you to figure out how you have coped with this life and where you could do with more experience, perhaps of a different kind.

Take, for instance, your birth chart. Take a good look at it, look at its strengths and its weaknesses, if possible get a knowledgeable friend to talk it over with you. Ask them honestly to point out which areas of character need work and which you can be proud of and polish even more. Have a look at other signs and other ascendants, place them in different houses and see what kind of personality they produce. Take it further and project a chart for the future with the planets in those houses you think would give you a chance to develop more quickly. Then look for a time in the future when the planets will be in the nearest positions to those in the chart you are projecting. It may be in fifty, a hundred, or three hundred years time. But fix your mind and your desire upon that time and keep it uppermost in your mind, especially during your last moments of earthly consciousness.

Take a look at your present environment and see what you can change, improve or reduce in a future life. Where do you live? Do you like it enough to return to this country, town or village? What about religion? What about colour and race? If you are a true Initiate you will not fall into the trap of preparing a fantasy future life made up of luxury and influence, but one that will advance your knowledge of Self and the universe in which you exist. If your present work is concerned with high finance, you might wish to look towards something more active and closer to nature. Are you a doctor? Then how about becoming an artist or an engineer. Then there's sex!! Which one?

You might say in answer to all this, how do I know I have a choice? Well, how do you know you don't have a choice? You will never know until the time comes, but that does not mean you cannot prepare for it and plan for it. Leaving it up to 'God', by whatever name you use, is not why humanity was conceived. You and I and everyone who has ever lived have been put here to learn self-reliance, self-discipline and self-knowledge, so let us at least try to follow through.

Write down what you decide, keep it by you, add and subtract as you think it through and hold it fast as you begin to cross the final barrier. If nothing else it will give you something to think about – after all, dying may be quite boring.

The King is Dead, Long Live the King

One thing you can be sure of is that as Time goes on the higher levels, you won't be dead for long! There is too much to do, too much to learn, and good Initiates are hard to find. Some people are back so fast it can make your head swim. Many young souls dying violently return with great speed. Sometimes a suicide may need to return to live out the span they rejected. Others aver with great determination that they to not intend to return at all. Well, good luck to you, just try saying *no* to the Lords of Karma and Destiny. Equally, there are people who hold to the idea that this is their last life, they have achieved all that is necessary and they are due to 'ascend' from the earth and shake its dust from their feet. Again, good luck, we would all like to believe we have reached that point in our personal evolution, but it is highly unlikely to say the least. Speaking for myself, it's going to be a long hard slog to that day!

Nobody pretends dying is easy, but then living is not always a bed of roses either. Go with humour and, if possible, a laugh and a joke. Oscar Wilde's last words, so I am told, were, 'Either that wallpaper goes or I do'. The wallpaper won. One late member of the present Royal dynasty ended with the curious statement, 'Bugger Bognor', which invites one's curiosity if nothing else.

One last piece of advice, think about your epitaph. After all, you deserve to have The Last Word.

Appendix 1

The Ur-Hekau Sceptre

This is one of the two instruments used in the ceremony of Opening the Mouth. It is a snake-like piece of wood with the top carved into a ram's head. See drawing below by courtesy of Billie John.

It can be made fairly easily from wood, particularly a piece

of matured ivy which often has a naturally curved shape. The ram's head addition can then be fashioned from either Fina Wax, or if you have skill enough, carved from a piece of Balsa wood and glued to the sceptre. The one I use has a base of ivy wood but I was lucky enough to find a silver ram's head of fair size in an old junk shop and added that to the wand.

The Adze

This is more difficult with regard to shape as you can see from the drawing below.

However it can be cut from thick card and coloured. This will be just as effective for the rite.

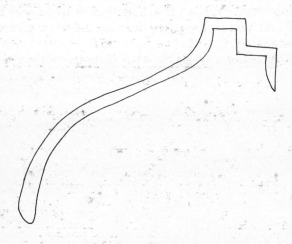

Appendix 2

Death by violence is, unfortunately, not infrequent in our modern world. When it happens it is usually without warning of any kind. For an Initiate there is really only one solution and that is to prepare for such an eventuality by making a 'death working' and time-sealing it with a password or symbol. This I have explained in my book *Highways of the Mind*. Make sure that there is someone who knows just what you wish to be done, make a will and update it whenever this is necessary. Arrange for your funeral, for a memorial service if you wish for this, and make certain that everything is as watertight as you can get it. You may wish, if death occurs abroad, for your remains to be brought home. This can be expensive so make sure you always carry adequate insurance. You may wish to be cremated there and then the ashes brought home. This will entail costs for cremation and carriage home.

With regard to what you can do on the inner levels, there will always be a certain amount of shock no matter how advanced you are in your studies. Do not even try to combat this, allow those who will most certainly arrive on the scene to help you. Go with them, do not look back. Your immediate concern is for healing of a type you can only obtain on the inner levels. You do not need the trauma of seeing your physical body in a mutilated condition or, if this is the case, the person responsible. Remember, if you can accept what has happened and if you can leave at once you are less likely to go through the horror and anger that wells up if you hang around. Uncontrolled anger at what you see as the cutting short of precious living time can alter the structure of Karmic debt. Once you have rested, healed and calmed down, you will be able to accept what has happened as just another in a long line of deaths and one from which you will be able to learn. Once the immediate shock is over you will be able to contact your family on the inner levels when they sleep. It will be far worse for them than for you.

On the physical level *never* try to contact a person who has gone over in this way until they have had time to adjust, otherwise you will hold them back from essential healing. Strive for a period of meditation and calm within yourself, anger, desire for revenge, blaming yourself, all these can disrupt much needed rest and recuperation for the one who has departed. Yes, it *is* difficult, almost impossible at times but try, because it is the best thing you can do for them. Healing thoughts of love and support are what they need. Contact the angelic forces, the Gods and the Devas, they will relay your thoughts.

Are there any rites for such times as these? Yes, there are, but they are best left for at least a lunar month before being worked. By then the ripples of violence will have died down and although the feelings and emotions are still running high the cutting edge has been taken off the grief. Unless the victim was a total unbeliever in any form of survival, or if they too were a part of the violence, something that is very unlikely, there *will* be beings there to help them. This is especially true of young people and children. Often the parent's grief is mixed up with other thoughts, 'I didn't say goodbye to them', or 'I shouted at him and he went off in a huff, I never had the chance to say I'm sorry', and '. . . it's her birthday next week, we have her present already wrapped up'. I do urge those going through such dreadful times to try and hang on to one thought: you have not lost them forever, when love is strong it binds people together beyond death.

The Rite

This is a rite for children and young people, teenagers of either sex. It requires four people and can be worked 28 days after death, or recovery of body. You need an altar covered with a white cloth, white flower heads or petals, a white candle at each quarter and a central altar light. Incense should be light in character, nothing heavy, and used in a thurible. Beside the

altar place a small tree seedling, a bowl of consecrated water
and a sprig of Rosemary to use as an asperge. At each quarter
lay on the altar a small photograph of the person. If possible
white robes, if not then light coloured clothing, nothing dark
should be worn.

Begin with the Summoning of the Archangels, moving from
East to South, to West and to North. Summon the Devas of
each quarter to the *left* side of the Archangels and the
Elemental Kings to the *right* side of the Archangels. (Use the
summonings given in the second part of the book.)

East: (lights candle from the altar light and opens East with
Pentacle) WE HAVE COME TOGETHER TO OFFER OUR
LOVE AND SUPPORT TO . . . AND TO THOSE LEFT
BEHIND IN THE PHYSICAL WORLD. WE HAVE
SUMMONED THE HOSTS OF HEAVEN FOR THIS
PURPOSE THAT THEY MAY WITNESS OUR RITE AND
RETURN TO . . . WITH WORD OF THE EVENT. (turns to
East with water and asperge) I STAND FOR THE MALE SIDE
OF THE FAMILY. LET THIS WATER SYMBOLIZE THEIR
TEARS, AS I CAST IT OVER THE EAST, LET . . . REST IN
THE LIGHT AND BE SUPPORTED BY OUR LOVE AND
OUR MEMORIES. RAPHAEL, AS YOU HEAL . . . I ASK
ALSO THAT YOUR HEALING POWER BE USED FOR
THOSE WHO MOURN, LEFT TO SORROW AND TO LIVE
ON WITHOUT THE SIGHT OF THEIR LOVED ONE. WE
PLACE . . . IN YOUR ARMS AND YIELD HER/HIM UP TO
YOU. CAST OUT FROM US BITTERNESS AND HATRED
AND ANGER, HELP US TO UNDERSTAND AND TO
ACCEPT. I YIELD UP THIS SYMBOL (takes photograph and
places it in the East) OF . . . TO RAPHAEL, THAT THE SOUL
MAY BE HEALED, TO PARALDA THAT THE ELEMENT OF
HER/HIS AIR BE RETURNED TO ITS NATURAL PLACE,
AND TO THE DEVAS OF THE EAST THAT HER/HIS
MEMORIES OF LIFE MAY BE PRESERVED. LET ALL THIS
BE SO.

South: (lights candle from altar light and opens South with
Pentacle) I STAND FOR THE BROTHERS AND SISTERS, THE
FAMILY AND THE FRIENDS OF . . . (turns with water,
asperges the South) LET THIS WATER SYMBOLIZE THEIR
TEARS AS I CAST IT OVER THE SOUTH. LET . . . REST IN
THE GLOW OF THE SETTING SUN AND KNOW

HER/HIMSELF TO BE SUPPORTED BY OUR LOVE AND
OUR MEMORIES. MICHAEL TAKE THE MEMORIES OF
PAIN AND FEAR, AND SORROW FROM OUR LOVED ONE
AND DISSOLVE THEM IN THE DIVINE FIRE. SHIELD . . .
FROM OUR GRIEF LEST SHE/HE FEELS DRAWN TO
RETURN TO THIS PLANE. WE PASS HER/HIM INTO YOUR
CARE AND UNDER YOUR PROTECTION. LET NO
BITTERNESS OR HATRED MAR THE HEALING, BUT LET
THE LESSON BE LEARNED AND ACCEPTED. I YIELD UP
THIS SYMBOL (takes photograph and places it in the South)
OF . . . TO MICHAEL THAT THE PAIN AND FEAR BE
EASED AWAY, TO DJINN THAT THE ELEMENT OF HER/HIS
FIRE BE RETURNED TO ITS NATURAL PLACE, AND TO
THE DEVAS OF THE SOUTH THAT THE FIRE OF HER/HIS
LOVE FOR US BE REMEMBERED. LET ALL THIS BE SO.

North: (lights candle from altar light and opens North with
Pentacle) I STAND FOR THE MOTHER WHO BORE THIS
CHILD AND WHOSE GRIEF RUNS WOMB DEEP. (turns
with water and asperges North) LET THIS WATER
SYMBOLIZE HER TEARS AS IT SINKS DOWN INTO THE
EARTH IN THE NORTH. LET HER DAUGHTER/SON REST
IN THE ARMS OF URIEL THERE TO SLEEP AND DREAM
OF THOSE LEFT BEHIND. URIEL HOLD THE CHILD
CLOSE AND BREATHE UPON ITS BROW AND DRIVE
AWAY ALL BUT THE MEMORIES OF LOVE AND JOY. THE
MOTHER PASSES HER CHILD INTO THY CARE. SHE
YIELDS UP HER GRIEF AND BITTERNESS TO THEE AND
ASKS FOR HEALING. THE MOTHER YIELDS UP THIS
SYMBOL OF HER CHILD (Takes photograph and places it in
North) TO THEE URIEL THAT IT MAY BE A LINK BETWEEN
THEM UNTIL THEY ARE REUNITED. TO GHOB, THAT THE
PHYSICAL FORM SHE CARRIED AND BORE MAY BE
RETURNED TO ITS NATURAL ELEMENTAL STATE OF
EARTH. TO THE DEVAS OF THE NORTH THAT THE
'MEMORY TREE' MAY GROW AND FLOURISH. LET ALL
THIS BE SO.

West: (Lights candle from altar light and open West with
Pentacle) I STAND FOR THE ANGEL OF DEATH INTO
WHOSE CARE THE CHILD HAS BEEN PASSED. ALL
HUMANITY HAS A TIME ALLOTTED TO THEM AND
BEYOND THAT TIME THEY MAY NOT PASS. MY TEARS
ARE JOINED TO YOURS, MY SORROW IS AS DEEP, MY

HEART AS HEAVY. THIS TASK WAS GIVEN TO ME IN THE BEGINNING OF TIME, I DID NOT SEEK IT. IN WHATEVER SHAPE AND FORM I COME, I COME AS FRIEND. I DO NOT CAUSE PAIN AND FEAR, I END IT AND FREE THE SOUL TO COME AGAIN OUT OF THE WEST. (takes photograph and circles the temple gathering up all the others, returns to West) I GATHER THIS CHILD TO MYSELF, THE BRIGHTNESS OF THE SPIRIT I RETURN TO GABRIEL TO BE MADE ANEW, THE ELEMENT OF WATER I RETURN TO NIXSA THAT IT MAY BE REFORMED IN THE OCEANS OF TIME AND SPACE. THE DEVAS OF THE WEST SHALL GUIDE THE BOAT OF THE SUN WHEREIN THE SOUL DEPARTS BEYOND THE FARTHEST SHORE. LET ALL THIS BE SO.

(The sapling is laid on the altar and blessed with water, censed, and consecrated to the memory of the departed. It is covered with the flowers and left overnight to be planted next day, the flowers should be scattered over the grave or placed around the roots of the sapling.)

East: . . ., THE EAST LETS YOU DEPART INTO THE LIGHT. (douses candle)

South: . . ., THE SOUTH LETS YOU DEPART INTO THE LIGHT. (douses candle)

North: . . ., THE NORTH LETS YOU DEPART INTO THE LIGHT. (douses candle)

West: . . ., THE WEST ACCEPTS YOU INTO THE LIGHT. WELCOME. (douses candle)

The Rite for Adults

This is a full rite either for a Lodge member or worked by the Lodge at the request of the family of an adult who has passed on as the result of an act of violence. There are four officers, and four who stand for the Elemental Kings, the Devas, the Archangels *or* the Four Winds of the Earth if the Lodge is pagan orientated, and for The Great Mother.

The altar is dressed in white with a photograph of the person in the centre. At the four quarters of the altar stands a lighted white candle. A thurible filled with any incense that pertains to the Great Mother, either in Her name of Isis, o

Binah, or The White Goddess. In the East the officer holds two
flowers, one red and one white. In the South the Officer holds
the Thurible, in the West the Officer holds a bowl of
consecrated water and a sprig of Rosemary. In the north the
Officer holds a bowl of mixed seeds. The representative of the
Archangels/Winds stand behind the Eastern officer. That of
the Elemental Kings behind the Southern officer, for the
Devas behind the Western officer, and for the Great Mother
behind the Northern officer.

Gt Mother: I HAVE RECEIVED BACK INTO MY CARE THE
BRIGHT SPIRIT OF . . . BUT THERE IS HEALING TO BE
DONE AND THE REMAINING LINKS TO EARTH MUST BE
SEVERED.
  Deva: THE EARTH WILL HOLD THE MEMORY OF . . .
AND WE OF THE DEVIC KINGDOM WILL SUSTAIN THAT
MEMORY.
  East: THE ELEMENTS THAT SUSTAINED THE PHYSICAL
BODY OF . . . SHALL BE RETURNED TO THEIR OWN
PLACE, AND THEY SHALL BE BLESSED FOR THEIR PART
IN THAT LIFE.
  Angels: THE PRIMAL SPARK OF . . . HAS ENRICHED THE
EARTH AND THE LIVES OF THOSE WHO KNEW
HER/HIM. FOR THIS THE SPIRIT SHALL BE BLESSED.
  East: TO THE EAST I TURN TO OPEN THE GATES OF THE
DAWN. (with the flowers makes pentacle) LET THE FOUR
ARCHANGELS OF THE PRESENCE/LET THE FOUR
WINDS OF THE EARTH STAND READY TO TAKE THE
SPIRIT OF . . . BEYOND THIS PLANE OF EARTH. I BLESS
AND HALLOW THE SPIRIT OF . . . I CALL THE LIGHT TO
ENFOLD AND HEAL HER/HIM AND IN THE FULLNESS
OF TIME I ASK THAT WE MEET AGAIN IN THE FLESH
AND RENEW OUR TIES.
  South: TO THE SOUTH I TURN TO OPEN THE GATES OF
NOON. (censes the South) LET THE MIGHTY MALACHIM,
THE GREAT KINGS OF THE ELEMENTS, STAND READY
TO RECEIVE EACH THEIR RIGHTFUL ELEMENT BACK
FROM THE BODY OF . . . LET THOSE ELEMENTS BE
BLESSED TO THE AMOUNT THEY ARE ABLE TO RECEIVE
FOR THEIR WORK. I BLESS AND HALLOW THE
CONSCIOUSNESS OF . . . AND CALL UPON THE LORDS
OF MIND TO HEAL THE HURT CAUSED BY THE EVENTS

OF DEATH. I ASK THAT WE SHALL MEET AGAIN IN ANOTHER TIME.

West: TO THE WEST I TURN TO OPEN THE GATES OF THE SETTING SUN (asperges the West) I CALL THE BRIGHT DEVAS TO WATCH OVER THE DREAMS OF . . . AND FILL THEM WITH PEACE AND SWEET MEMORIES. I BLESS AND HALLOW THE THOUGHTS AND THE PERSONALITY OF . . . AND CALL UPON THE DEVAS TO PRESERVE THAT KNOWLEDGE WHICH SHE/HE WENT OVER, THAT IT MAY BE RETURNED TO HER/HIM IN A FUTURE LIFE. I ASK THAT WE MAY RENEW OUR FRIENDSHIP AT THAT TIME.

North: TO THE NORTH I TURN TO OPEN THE GATES OF PERSEPHONE AND THE DARK MOON. (Offers the bowl of seeds to North) I INVOKE THE MIGHTY PRESENCE OF THE GREAT MOTHER. BINAH AND ISIS, ARADIA AND INNANA ARE BUT SOME OF YOUR NAMES. COME TO US, COMFORT US, EASE THE PAIN AND SORROW IN THE HEARTS OF THOSE WHO HAVE LOVED AND LOST AS YOU HAVE EASED THE PAIN AND FEAR FROM THE HEART AND MIND OF . . . ENFOLD HER/HIM WE PRAY AND COMFORT HER/HIM. LET THE DREAMS OF NIGHT BRING US ALL TOGETHER ONCE MORE. BLESS US ALL WITH THY STRENGTH COMFORT AND UNDERSTANDING.

East: (Takes candle and processes round the altar stopping at the four quarters beginning with the East) WITH THE LIGHT OF THE HIGHER WORLDS I CAST AWAY THE SHADOW OF DARK MEMORIES FROM THE SOUL OF . . . (to South) WITH THE LIGHT OF CLEAR SEEING I CAST AWAY THE FEAR FROM THE SOUL OF . . . (to West) WITH THE LIGHT OF KNOWLEDGE I CAST AWAY PAIN AND SUFFERING FROM THE SOUL OF . . . (to North) WITH THE LIGHT OF UNDERSTANDING I CAST AWAY BITTERNESS FROM THE SOUL OF . . . PEACE, PEACE AND PEACE TO YOU.

South: (Takes candle and repeats the moves beginning in the South) WITH THE FIRE OF LOVE I CAST AWAY REGRET FROM THE SOUL OF . . . WITH THE FIRE OF WISDOM CAST AWAY HATRED FROM THE SOUL OF . . . WITH THE FIRE OF SELF DISCIPLINE I CAST AWAY THE DESIRE FOR REVENGE FROM THE SOUL OF . . . WITH THE FIRE O

PURE SPIRIT I BESEECH THE SOUL OF . . . TO NEGATE ALL KARMIC DEBTS OWED TO HER/HIM BY OTHERS THAT THE SAME OFFER MADE BE MADE TO HER/HIM. THUS WILL ALL BE MADE TRUE. LOVE, LOVE, AND LOVE TO YOU.

West: (Takes candle and repeats moves as above beginning in the West) WITH THE FLAME OF INTUITION I FILL THE SOUL OF . . . WITH KNOWLEDGE. WITH THE FLAME OF FAR MEMORY I FILL THE SOUL OF . . . WITH THE WISDOM OF HER/HIS PAST LIVES. WITH THE FLAME OF DESIRE I FILL THE SOUL OF . . . WITH EAGERNESS FOR A NEW INCARNATION. WITH THE FLAME OF CREATION I FILL THE SOUL OF . . . WITH ENERGY AND STRENGTH WHEN THE NEW LIFE SHALL BEGIN. WISDOM, WISDOM, AND WISDOM TO YOU.

North: (Takes candle and repeats moves as above beginning with the North) WITH THE RAY OF THE LORDS OF FLAME I BLESS THE SOUL OF . . . WITH THEIR POWERS. WITH THE RAY OF THE LORDS OF FORM I BLESS THE SOUL OF . . . WITH THEIR POWERS. WITH THE RAY OF THE LORDS OF MIND I BLESS THE SOUL OF . . . WITH THEIR POWERS. LIGHT, LOVE, WISDOM AND UNDERSTANDING TO YOU NOW AND IN THE AGES TO COME.

East: I BID THE POWERS OF THE EAST TO DEPART IN PEACE.

South: I BID THE POWERS OF THE SOUTH TO DEPART IN PEACE.

West: I BID THE POWERS OF THE WEST TO DEPART IN PEACE.

North: I BID THE POWERS OF THE NORTH TO DEPART IN PEACE.

All: WE BID FAREWELL TO YOU . . . UNTIL WE SHALL MEET AGAIN IN THE LIGHT.

Appendix 3

Prayers for the Dead

Christian Tradition

'I am the resurrection and the life, saith the Lord: he that believéth in me, though he were dead, yet shall he live and whosoever liveth and believeth in me shall never die.'

We brought nothing into this world, and it is certain we can carry nothing out. The Lord gave and the Lord hath taken away; blessed be the name of the Lord.

'Lord thou hast been our refuge: from one generation to another. Before the mountains were brought forth, or ever the earth and the world were made thou art God from everlasting, world without end.'

Psalms

Psalm number 9. Psalm 11. Psalm 23. Psalm 24. Psalm 27. Psalm 63.

Qabalistic Tradition

Thou art the Lord of Hosts and Geburah is thy name. The body has been cast away for it no longer has a place upon the earth. Yea it shall be given back to the earth, or to the sea or to the air. That of which it was made has been set asunder. The soul riseth upon the wind and shall return to the Lord of Hosts. Ever and ever shall the soul praise the Eternal Crown and upon the Foundation shall the new life be made manifest.

Lift up my soul from the red earth that I may praise Adonai the Lord and King of earth. Set my feet upon the path that leads to the Foundation of the world that I may praise the Almighty living God. Let me be made manifest in the mind of the Most High and raised up to the great Star of Heaven wherein are set the Holy Creatures of Da'ath. Yea I shall become one with the White Head of Kether and I shall be as I shall be forever.

I am the child of Binah the sorrowful, from Marah the bitter sea did I emerge and to that great and unknowable source shall I return. Let the Seraphim and Cherubim raise me up that I may behold the Sun behind the Sun and know that which made me face to face in the light of a new dawning.

Jewish Tradition
See the TORAH, Psalms of David.

Wiccan and Pagan
Sweet Persephone call to me and raise me from the sweet earth that covers me that I may follow you into the realm of Hades. Bind me with thy hair and sing me sweet songs of peaceful rest. Let me sleep in the arms of death until I am called once more to the earth and to life.

Behond the Lord of Hades has summoned me and I await his chariot. Great is the Lord of the Underworld and I shall dwell in the Fields of Elysium among the asphodel until my time shall come again. The earth trembles, he comes, he comes, and I am ready.

White Lady, sweet Aradia lead me gently along the moon path to freedom and to the great Moon Mother. Let me rest peacefully after the strife and struggle of human life. I have been faithful to thee and to thy worship. The sabbats and the esbats have I kept and as the seasons changed I made the offerings as decreed. Ease my passing Great Goddess and send the moon boat to take me to my rest.

Egyptian Tradition
Behold my sun has come to its setting and there is no more life in me. I call beyond dying sun to Ra in his glory. Come, great Ones send thy boat for me. Let me depart to Amenti.

Osiris, behond thy son/daughter and thy servants as we prepare the body for its rest. Let the arms of thy mother Nuit enfold the justified one that they may pass over the bridge between the worlds. Hail Osiris, lord of Amenti thy name is in our mouths. Hail Isis Mother of the Sun Child hold the departed in thy womb that he/she may be reborn.

Prayer to Clean and Concecrate Salt and Water

Water

Make the equal armed cross over the container and say 'Creature of water by the moon that rules thee I cast out from thee all that is impure and call in all that is pure and clean, so shall it be as I have said.'

Salt

Make the equal armed cross over the container and say, 'Creature of salt, by the earth that claims thee I cast out from thee all that is impure and call in all that is pure and clean, so shall it be as I have said.'

Bibliography

Appelbaum, D. *Real Philosophy* Arkana, 1990.
Ashcroft-Nowicki, D. *Highways of the Mind* The Aquarian Press, 1987.
– *Ritual Magic Workbook* The Aquarian Press, 1986.
– (ed) *The Forgotten Mage* The Aquarian Press, 1986.
– *The Sacred Cord Meditations* The Aquarian Press, 1990.
Budge, Wallis, E.A. *The Egyptian Book of the Dead* Dover, 1967.
Caine, R.H. *Annals of the Sacred Isle* Cecil Palmer, 1926.
Campbell, J. (ed) *The Mysteries* Eranons Yearbooks Vol 2, Bollingen, 1955.
Chaney, E. *The Mystery of Death and Dying* Weiser,1988.
Chogyam Trungpa, *The Tibetan Book of the Dead* Shambhala, 1987.
Dennis, J. T. *The Burden of Isis* Wisdom of the East Series, 1918.
Farr, F. *Egyptian Magic* The Aquarian Press, 1982.
Feinstein, D. and Elliott Mayo, P. *Rituals for Living and Dying* HarperCollins, 1990
Fortune, D. *Through the Gates of Death* The Aquarian Press, 1968
Gorer, G. *Death, Grief and Mourning* The Cresset Press, 1965.
Hope, M. *Ancient Egypt: The Sirius Connection* Element, 1990.
Jones, B. *Design for Death* André Deutsch, 1967.
Liturgy of the Liberal Catholic Church.
Pace, M.M. *Wrapped for Eternity* Lutterworth Press, 1977.
Ellis N. Phanes (trans) *Awakening Osiris: The Egyptian Book of the Dead* 1988.
Radford, E. and M. *Encyclopaedia of Superstitions* Rider, 1947.
Rainwater, J. *Self Therapy* Crucible, 1979.
Spence, Lewis *Second Sight, its History and Origins* Rider, 1951.
The Instruction of Ra-Hotep Wisdom of the East series, 1906.

Watts, Alan *Myth and Ritual in Christianity* Thames and Hudson, 1954.

Wilkinson, Sir J. Gardner *The Ancient Egyptians* Studio Editions, 1990.

The Apocrphya.

The Oxford Book of Mystical Verse.

The Holy Bible.

Index